ENDORSEM

There is a culture war over the goodness of God and those who dare to unveil the reality of our reconciled union are in the crosshairs. Steve Smothers is standing at the forefront of this conversation with *Living Loved*. If Steve's first book challenged your view of God, this book will take that same lens and challenge your view of YOU. If we have any work to do on this side of the cross it's to let go of the lies that we've believed about ourselves to see how the Father sees us. *Living Loved* asks all the right questions, which are the hard ones. By the end of the book you will hopefully have done the work of shedding the fear that blinds so many to the goodness and grace of a God who won't even let you change how He feels about you.

— Bill Vanderbush,
Speaker and Author of *Reckless Grace*

I can't think of a more inviting subject than this, or a book so beautifully complete in covering the true issues of discipleship. Summed up in a few words, in *Living Loved*, Steve has opened a door to the master secret of discipleship: Receiving his love and giving it away! Well done, Steve!

— Jack Taylor,
President Dimensions Ministries and Author of *Cosmic Initiative*

In *Living Loved*, Steve takes the enormous concepts of "Living on the Right Side of the Cross" and "Better Covenant Discipleship" and makes them easily and clearly accessible to us all. Whether you're trying to wrap your mind around practical implications of the cross and the new covenant or looking for tools for disciple-making this book is a must read.

— **Joel Lowry,**
Lead Pastor of Sozo Church San Marcos

In the first chapter of *Living Loved*, Steve writes how at age 32 his life was changed: "Little did I realize, Blackaby's *Experiencing God: Knowing and Doing the Will of God* was about to change my life. It was exactly what I needed to read at this transitional time in my life." By God's grace, Steve's experience became reality for me in 2012 as Steve mentored me through the study of *Experiencing God*. It is so interesting that the title of Steve's newest book *Living Loved,* are the words I use when sharing the transition God made in my life through Steve. I was so excited to learn that God is continuing His work through Steve via the Better Covenant Series. In *Living Loved,* as with the first book in the series, *Seeing Through A Better Lens,* God uses Steve's knowledge, experience and giftedness as a visionary teacher to provide readers an impactful resource for living loved, living full, and living free.

— **Marvin Williams**
Entrepreneur and Disciple Maker

Thanks to advancements in the international adoption process I was given the opportunity to become a father to my three adopted children long before they had the chance of meeting me. They did not yet understand I had already said "yes" to loving them; they did not know I had promised to give them the best life I could provide. I knew their faces, their stories, their past hardships and the conditions they were facing in their orphanages. I had first-hand insight into how they lived, what brought them joy, and what they needed to thrive. How paradoxical that I could know so much about these children and they, in turn, were not even aware that they had a father; that they were no longer orphans. The knowledge that they had a home began to set in the first moment when we were united. It is hard to explain what it was like when we locked eyes for the first time and embraced each other. They were finally able to experience what I had known all along– they were loved and a better life awaited them.

How heart-breaking that we can be cognizant of God's love, but unaware that we are experiencing life like an untethered orphan. The truth is, it is through lived experiences that teaching comes alive and leads us to thrive. In *Living Loved*, Steve Smothers takes us from knowing about God to experiencing His love and the life awaiting us. Living Loved reveals how the Holy Spirit desires to take us on the shortest, yet most profound journey a child of God can ever take – the journey from the head to the heart. Through this book, I pray you will lock eyes with Jesus in a fresh new way. I pray you will experience the embrace of our loving Heavenly Father who has provided more for you, far beyond your current understanding of His love. At the end of this encounter, I believe you will agree: we don't have to live as orphans any more!

— **Jason Lohse**
Entrepreneur, Author and Disciple Maker

Steve Smothers has long had a grace for pushing envelopes. He continues that tradition with *Living Loved.* Steve implores readers to leave behind thinking of union with God as merely an idea. He lays out something much more grand— embodied union with God through experience! Anyone who leans into this book will be met with challenging truth, empowering grace, and a new lens.

— Jarrett Martin,
Marketplace Missionary

There are two characteristics of a great teacher. First, the best teachers are not necessarily the ones with "book smarts." They are the ones who teach from what they have experienced. They draw from a deep well of experiences that they have gained over many years of "pressing in." They are not satisfied with a surface level understanding of a subject, but instead have accepted the invitation to go deep. Yet all of this means nothing if they can't communicate what they have experienced.

Steve Smothers is just that, a great teacher and extremely gifted communicator. Drawing from a well that is over three decades deep, Steve masterfully communicates what the Father has revealed to him in *Living Loved.* In this book Steve peals back what man's religion has distorted, primarily Dad's love. Steve has an uncanny ability to take scripture, break it down and communicate what God intended us to know about Him and His love for us. By giving us a proper lens, Steve reveals the simple fact that we were designed to receive the Father's unending, abundant love that leads to a full life of freedom. This fabulous book will also give you the tools to disciple others in living on the "right side of the cross." Take your time reading this book and enjoy a long cool drink from a deep well.

— Tom Cavazos,
Airline Pilot and Missions Coordinator Sozo Church San Marcos

I love Pastor Steve Smothers' heart for the Kingdom of God and for reaching people for Christ. He is a visionary when it comes to making disciples. As one discipled by him, I have experienced first-hand his commitment and desire for the Church to become all God intended. I'm excited that he has shared in *Living Loved* the things he has learned while faithfully allowing God to work through him to grow disciples, leaders and churches through the years. This book contains wisdom, insights and principles that I believe can equip any believer to help another person on their faith journey and help the Church to bring the love, life and freedom of Jesus to the people of its community.

— **Norman Garcia,**
Pastor of Gateway Church Dripping Springs

I first met Steve at a regional gathering of leaders in 2015. Several months later, we would gather in a smaller group to discuss working together to bring the Kingdom within our Region. That day, I heard the Lord say "Steve is my gift to this region as a teacher." I strongly believe that the Lord is raising up Five-Fold Leaders to equip and build up the Body of Christ for a great harvest. Steve is a gifted teacher who communicates the Biblical truth of the Kingdom in a way that transforms, not just informs. *Living Loved* is a life giving and empowering tool for making disciples. I especially love the activations and reflections which cause the reader to actively engage and experience God relationally. This is a must for every believer.

— **Jay Moeller,**
Pastor of Legacy Church New Braunfels

Steve Smothers is a gifted teacher and author with the ability to convey truths about God and unpack concepts throughout scripture that are not only revelatory, but also bring immense freedom to the reader. As a mentee of Steve's for years, I can honestly say that his approach to the scriptures and his heart for New Covenant discipleship have shaped my life and leadership more than anyone else. Steve has given me one of the greatest gifts I have ever received, a better lens through which to see God, Scripture, life and ministry.

My passion for discipleship and desire to see God move have led me to countless discipleship guides, strategies, methods and systems. You name it, I've tried it. As I've grown in my understanding of this reality that Steve calls, "life on the right side of the cross," I have struggled marrying the concept of New Covenant Living with the desire to see a real movement of multiplying disciples. Steve's perspective, content and lens for discipleship laid out in this book is like a fresh drink of cold water. As a college pastor, this book has become vital in creating a framework for discipling young people. Through years of college ministry I've learned that young people don't just need answers to their questions, they need a better lens to see through. This book is just that. This book will give you a fresh perspective of how to approach the scriptures, how to live a new covenant lifestyle and how to disciple others into that same reality.

— **Dustin West,**
College Pastor of Sozo Church San Marcos

I've been taught and discipled by Steve for about five years now. His relationship in my life is one of a father to a son. Steve Smothers is an incredible leader, a great presenter of Better Covenant Theology, and an even better friend. This book is an overflow of his heart to see the ends of the earth reached with the love of our Father. Reading *Living Loved* will stir a passion in your heart to see sons and daughters restored to their identity and purpose, while empowering you to partner with Father in the ministry of reconciliation (2 Corinthians 5). I will utilize this material for years as I obey our Lord's command to make disciples of all nations.

— Justin Johnson,
College Student and Disciple Maker

Living Loved
Copyright © 2020 Steve K. Smothers

Bracketed text within Scripture quotations is the author's emphasis.

All Scripture quotations, unless otherwise indicated, are taken from the Holy Bible, New International Version®, NIV®. Copyright ©1973, 1978, 1984, 2011 by Biblica, Inc.™ Used by permission of Zondervan. All rights reserved worldwide. www.zondervan.comThe "NIV" and "New International Version" are trademarks registered in the United States Patent and Trademark Office by Biblica, Inc.™

Other scripture quotations are from:

Scripture quotations marked TPT are from The Passion Translation®. Copyright © 2017, 2018 by Passion & Fire Ministries, Inc. Used by permission. All rights reserved. ThePassionTranslation.com.

Scripture quotations marked (ESV) are from The ESV® Bible (The Holy Bible, English Standard Version®), copyright © 2001 by Crossway, a publishing ministry of Good News Publishers. Used by permission. All rights reserved.

Scripture quotations taken from the New American Standard Bible® (NASB), Copyright © 1960, 1962, 1963, 1968, 1971, 1972, 1973, 1975, 1977, 1995 by The Lockman Foundation
Used by permission. www.Lockman.org

Scripture taken from the New King James Version. Copyright © 1982 by Thomas Nelson, Inc. Used by permission. All rights reserved.

ISBN: 978-1-7330596-2-6 (*paperback*)

Ryan Smothers — Editor, cover and interior design
Beth Smothers — Associate editor, interior design
Karen Steinmann — Technical editor
Joel Lowry — Featured contributor (chapter 14)

Printed in the United States of America

Published by BETTER COVENANT LIVING, LLC
San Marcos, Texas, USA
Visit BetterCovenantLiving.com

LIVING LOVED

Living Full. Living Free

STEVE K. SMOTHERS

CONTENTS

THE BETTER COVENANT

If you have health insurance, it is helpful to be familiar with the benefits of your policy. If you do not know those benefits, you won't take advantage of them, and you may end up paying for something that the policy covers.

The same is true of new covenant believers who are unaware of just how much better the new covenant in Christ is than the old (Mosaic) covenant. Many Christians are ignorant of the great benefits that they enjoy in Jesus Christ and, as a result, the enemy takes advantage of them. They end up "paying" for things that are "already in the policy (new covenant)"! So using the analogies of scripture—instead of knowing the glorious privileges of being children of the free woman, they live in slavery as children of the bondwoman (Gal. 4:30-31).

The author of Hebrews contrasts the old and new covenants to demonstrate the superiority of the new covenant that Christ enacted through His blood.

Throughout Hebrews 8-10 he argues:

...the new covenant is better than the old covenant because it is enacted on better promises, by a better high priest through a better (once-for-all) sacrifice.

Hebrews 8:6-7 is a good summary:

"...the ministry Jesus has received is as superior to theirs (old covenant high priests) as the covenant of which he is mediator is superior to the old one, since the new covenant is established on better promises."

We must understand that the new covenant is radically different from the old covenant that Israel did not keep (8:7-9). Clearly, the emphasis here is on *discontinuity*, not on continuity. God is drawing a sharp distinction between the failure of the old covenant and the certain success of the new covenant.

• The old covenant could not impart spiritual life, but the new covenant does (*Galatians 3:21; 2 Corinthians 3:6*).

• The purpose of the old covenant law was to define and magnify our sinfulness, so that we would be drawn to faith in Christ. The new covenant focuses on our new identity in Christ (*Galatians 3:19-24; Romans 5:20; 2 Corinthians 5:17*).

- The old covenant law led to bondage, whereas the new covenant leads to freedom (*Galatians 4:21-5:1*).

- The old covenant law was external and thus did not supply the power to meet its demands, whereas the new covenant is internal and supplies authority, power and life (*Romans 8:3-4*).

- The old covenant law could not provide full and complete forgiveness of sins, but the new covenant does (*Hebrews 9:9; 10:1-4, 10*).

- The old covenant law was based on an inferior priesthood, but the new covenant is based on the superior priesthood of Jesus (*Hebrews 7:11—8:6*).

- The old covenant law did not bring everyone under it to know the Lord personally, but the new covenant does (*Hebrews 8:11*).

- The old covenant law was limited largely to one physical nation, whereas the new covenant extends to all people (*Acts 2:17-18; Romans 15:8-12*).

- The old covenant law kept worshipers at a distance from God because of His holiness and their sinfulness, whereas the new covenant invites us to draw near to God (*Hebrews 4:16; 7:19; 10:22*).

The old covenant law served a temporary function. It is now obsolete and outdated, whereas the new covenant is both current and eternal (*Galatians 3:19-25; Hebrews 8:13; 9:9-12; 13:20*).

— **Steven J. Cole,**
Pastor of Flagstaff Christian Fellowship
From *Better Covenant,* lesson 24*

Cole's biblical overview offers a good explanation of why the language of new covenant and better covenant is used interchangeably throughout this book. Those who study theology will recognize that there is actually a difference between New Covenant Theology and Better Covenant Theology, but that is beyond the scope of this book.

01
EXPERIENCING GOD
Hearing God: Stepping into His Adventure

Disciple-making has long been a high value for me as a follower of Jesus. I must admit, however, that I have undergone quite an evolution in my understanding of what it means to be a New Covenant disciple of Jesus.

As a 19-year-old college student, being a disciple and making disciples of Jesus meant living a disciplined life, obeying *all* the rules, and being zealous to tell everyone I met about Jesus. Though highly motivated by self-effort, being a disciple of Jesus with my radical college comrades was real, raw, and organic. We built our relationships around the purpose of "sharpening" one another.

Looking back, I now realize that with all our really good intentions, we were missing something. Though we felt connected to Jesus and each other, and experienced a true sense of belonging and inclusion, our spiritual family was missing its *parents.* We had no spiritual dads or moms to help us process life and guide us through the new seasons of life we were encountering. Without spiritual parents, we more often resembled an orphanage than a family.

We certainly had the Holy Spirit to guide us, but we also needed the security and wisdom of the larger family of God. Most of our unfortunate outcomes were the result of us "pooling our collective ignorance" and coming up with a half-baked plan (that seemed perfectly logical to us at the time).

As a youth pastor in my twenties, I sought to learn all I could about making disciples of Jesus. I tried every program that came on the market. But with each new, innovative plan, I became increasingly disillusioned. *I would later learn that "disillusion" can be the beginning of breakthrough!* Dis-illusion means "to be free from illusion." Once the illusion is removed, then the authentic can emerge.

> **Disillusion can be the beginning of breakthrough! Dis-illusion means "to be free from illusion."**

GOD AT WORK

A major shift that significantly enlarged my understanding of discipleship began the first week of July 1994. At that time, I was a 32-year-old pastor at

Crossroads Baptist Church in southeast Austin. I had been in dialogue with my friend Rob about starting a new church in Dripping Springs, Texas.

I was confused about what I should do and needed to get away to clear my head and seek God's direction. My plan was to go see my parents, spend some time at the ranch, and pop a few firecrackers on July 4th. As I was leaving my office, I felt prompted to pick up a workbook that had been given to me by Jason, one of my spiritual sons, who had heard the author Henry Blackaby speak at his college. Jason said, "You gotta read this book; this guy is saying stuff that you have been saying over the years, only he says it a whole lot better."

Little did I realize, Blackaby's *Experiencing God: Knowing and Doing the Will of God* was about to change my life. It was exactly what I needed to read at this transitional time in my life.

For the next several days, I read *Experiencing God* and prayed about what my next season in ministry would hold. One afternoon while I was out prayer-walking in downtown Hallettsville, where my parents lived, I felt as if I were having an actual conversation with God. I felt Him directing me to start an *Experiencing God* group with some men. I naturally assumed that meant some men from the church I pastored, but I soon found out that God had bigger plans for me.

The thesis of *Experiencing God* is that one can actually hear the voice of God and join Him where He is already at work. So I decided to begin "experiencing God" by seeking out His agenda, not mine. Amazingly, the Holy Spirit brought the names and faces of five men to mind. All five were pastors from Austin. Each was from a different denominational background and did not know the other pastors very well. I love God's sense of humor.

When I got back to Austin, I immediately began to set up meetings with each pastor, still wondering what their response would be. I first met with Lester, who was the leader of a network of house churches. Lester had been a spiritual mentor and source of great encouragement to me. We met for lunch, and after some small talk, I mentioned to Lester that I had a specific purpose in our meeting. He nodded and calmly reached into his briefcase. "Before we start, I have something I want to show you," he said. To my surprise, Lester brought out two copies of *Experiencing God*. My confidence was soaring—truly God was at work.

Next, I met with Ken, the pastor of a Baptist church. I didn't really know Ken all that well but thought he might agree to be a part of the group since we were both Baptists. I met Ken at his office, and as we chatted, I noticed some *Experiencing God* videotapes (this was 1994) on his shelf. As we began to dialogue, Ken became emotional, sharing that he had always wanted to do an *Experiencing God* discipleship group but had never been able to motivate anyone in his church to make the daily study commitment and weekly two-hour group requirement. The more we talked, the more impressed I felt to ask Ken to facilitate our group. Ken gratefully said "yes." God was already at work.

The next guy I met with was Bernie. He and I had been hanging out together, and I loved his raw passion, theological mind, and sense of humor. Just a few years earlier, Bernie had been involved with a hyper-control discipleship movement, so I was unsure what his response would be. Once again, Bernie acknowledged that God had preceded my invitation and that he was desirous of a group of pastors with whom he could be real. So the group was beginning to take shape: a house church guy, a Baptist, a Cajun charismatic (Bernie's last name is Boudreaux), and a Bapti-costal (that's me).

James was the next pastor on my list. He was a former missionary to Japan and now served as the lead teacher of an Independent church that was formed during the Jesus Movement. Again, God had gone before me, and James said "yes" to joining our pastors' group.

The fifth pastor I approached was Big Don. Don looked more like a bouncer than a pastor. Truthfully, Don asked me if he could join the group. He was the new pastor of a small, country Baptist church that was, as he so eloquently put it, "stuck in a time warp." He needed a safe place to share his honest feelings and receive healing. I could think of no better place than our *Experiencing God* pastors' group.

I have a confession to make. I was so euphoric over the response of the five pastors whom the Holy Spirit had put on my heart, that I took matters into my own hands and invited a sixth pastor. I was confident that he would join our group. I mean, we had a similar background, he had availability to meet with us, and he seemed like a natural fit with the group. To my amazement, he said "no." Once again, I was getting the message: God wanted me to join His agenda, not the other way around. He would bless only what He initiates and energizes. Philippians 2:13 soon became a guiding verse: *"It is God who works in you both to will and to do for His good pleasure."*

What started out as a thirteen-week study, ended up lasting over six months. With us seldom sticking to the curriculum, most weeks consisted of a healthy combination of laughing, passionate sharing, and an occasional tear or two. There was one constant, however: our *Experiencing God* group was our weekly **"safe place."** It became a parenthesis in our busy week, where for two-plus hours we could let our hair down and freely share our honest feelings, dreams, hurts, and struggles without fear of shame or judgment. Our EG group was a place of sanctuary where we could receive care, comfort, and support. It was a place where vulnerability was not only encouraged, but applauded—a place of both invitation and challenge!

I think the phrase *mutual encouragement* best describes what this group offered me. We all need to be told, "You can do this; you have what it takes!" **Encouragement means *"to give courage."*** We all need a safe place to give and receive courage. We all need a safe place to give and receive support, confidence, and hope.

> We all need to be told, "You can do this; you have what it takes!"

I will never forget the simple yet profound lessons learned from this mutual disciple-making experience. They are summarized in these **7 Realities of Experiencing God**:

❶ God is always at work around you.

❷ God pursues a continuing love relationship with you that is real and personal.

❸ God invites you to become involved with Him in His work.

❹ God speaks by the Holy Spirit through the Bible, prayer, people, circumstances (and more) to reveal Himself, His purposes, and His ways.

❺ God's invitation for you to work with Him always leads you to a crisis of belief that requires faith and action.

❻ You must make major adjustments in your life to join God in what He is doing.

❼ You come to know God by experience as you obey Him, and He accomplishes His work through you.[1]

These seven realities of experiencing God that I learned and shared with my five brothers in Christ have forever shaped and guided my life, but information alone will not transform a life. These realities, coupled with the intentionality to create a safe place (culture) where vulnerability and honesty are encouraged, are vital to experiencing authentic Kingdom-discipleship.

> We all need a safe place to give and receive courage, support, confidence and hope.

Our six months of brotherhood culminated in a wonderful six-church celebration. *Each pastor and his church joined together* at the host Baptist church for a potluck meal and evening of celebration. There were powerful stories and testimonies from each pastor as well as church members who had been impacted by the positive "change they saw in their pastor." There was singing of every variety and style. There was choreographed and improvised dancing (yes, in the Baptist church). There was even a water baptism.

Here's an excerpt from a letter I received from pastor Bernie Boudreaux on March 1, 1995, following our six-church celebration:

> Dear Steve,
>
> Well, big guy, Sunday night was because of what you started. Are you proud of yourself? Everybody's life is all messed up because of that ol' book. I hope you're happy! Because I am. My life has changed in every area and is progressively getting better. We've all changed so much over the last six months. When I saw the guys on Sunday, they all looked like joyous new Christians.

Truthfully, the result of our pastors' group was not because of much that I did. It's just what happens when a desperate pastor endeavors to trust God. It's just what happens when a mixed assortment of fish swim together in the waters of the Kingdom (Matthew 13:47). But beware, as Bernie testified—risking to join God in His

Kingdom adventure will "mess you up"—in the best sort of way!

THE REST OF THE STORY

Over the course of our six-month pastors' *Experiencing God* group, the Lord made it clear to my wife Lesa and me that our family was to move to Dripping Springs to start a new church. In fact, we made the move in the middle of the fourth month of our *Experiencing God* group.

Each week I would share with my pastor friends another fresh "crisis of belief" that I was facing in my transition to Dripping Springs. And each week my band of brothers would pray with me, encourage me, and help me discern God's leading and the adjustments I needed to make in my life to join God in what He was doing.

As a first-time church planter, I had several "crises of belief," but by far, my greatest fear was, "How am I gonna sell my current modular home and relocate to a much more expensive area?" And if that was not a large enough faith obstacle, I also fretted over how I would make this move with no actual salary. This was a faith venture that would require the wisdom and direction of God. My only *given* was that Lesa and I and my friend Rob had heard God say, "Go to Dripping!"

One by one, each of my pastor friends confirmed that decision, and together we prayed and waited for the Holy Spirit's direction. **Realities 3–6** *(see page 12)* were being lived out weekly as we *experienced God's presence and voice together.* The amazing thing is that *each of us* was experiencing the same rekindling of our faith. For some it was a call to renewal in marriage and/ or family. For others it was repentance (aligning with the mind of God) over wrong thinking, prejudices, and practices. Clearly, all of us were experiencing fresh faith

> Risking to join God in His Kingdom adventure will "mess you up— in the best sort of way!"

for a much larger and inclusive Kingdom of God than we had ever encountered or imagined. No longer was ministry primarily about preserving or growing the churches we served; instead, we were now beginning to focus on the larger issue of the Kingdom of God. We now began to see the Church, in all of its many expressions, not as the endgame, but as an agent of the Kingdom.

Now, the rest of *my* story. As I was searching for a buyer for our home and seeking ways to either raise financial support or get a job to support my new role as a church planter, a friend recommended that I meet with a gentleman who had experience in fundraising. Little did I realize, this God-orchestrated meeting would change the course of my life.

My friend introduced me to John (not his real name), and the conversation began something like this: "When I was told we were meeting, **God immediately began to show me things regarding you**," John said, and then paused. "I want you to know this isn't usual for me . . . I'm really not very prophetic . . . This never happens to me." As he spoke, I was amazed at the accuracy and insight of his words. Finally, John said, "God told me to support you. So, what do you need?"

I was stunned! I asked him to explain what he meant. After all, I thought our meeting was supposed to be about him sharing with me the "how-to" of ministry fundraising. He smiled and continued, "How much money are you going to need each month to meet your financial needs? God said I'm supposed to support you!" I sat there in shock as I processed what he was saying. As I pondered my answer, John smiled and continued, "This offer of support will cease in the event of any of the following three things: One, if you get in the flesh and go off the deep end—the deal is off. Two, if I get in the flesh and go off the deep end—the deal is likely over . . . and that's incentive for you to regularly pray for me! And

> **What is your crisis of belief?**

three, when the church is able to support you and we both agree the healthiest course is for me to withdraw support—then I'll do so."

As I traveled home to my modest modular home in Del Valle to share the events of the day with Lesa, I was overwhelmed with gratitude! God had invited me to join Him in His work and was now providing for His initiative in the most unfathomable way. I couldn't wait to share how Papa had answered *our* prayers! And true to His word, God used John to support the Smothers family over the first few years of the existence of Dripping Springs Community Fellowship, until the church was able to fully support us.

This is just one of many "God at work" testimonies from our *Experiencing God* group. Over the next 19 years that I pastored Community Fellowship, I would receive fuller revelation of New Covenant discipleship, but the message of Kingdom-discipleship and unity among the *one Church* of our city would become the foundation and priority of all we did in Dripping Springs.

Today, more than 25 years later, and as a senior leader of a church in San Marcos, Texas, I still ask myself the following four questions.

GRACE REFLECTIONS
Journaling My Thoughts

1. Where is God at work around me?

2. Where is He inviting me to join Him?

3. What is my current crisis of belief (that will require faith and action)?

4. What adjustments is God requiring me to make in order to join Him in what He is doing?

02
SEEING THROUGH
A BETTER LENS
Making Sense of the Bible

"I've got to be me! I can't fake it anymore; I've just got to be who I am."

Working with college students in a city with a large university, I hear this statement all the time. There is a cry to be understood and valued for *who I am,* not merely for what I do or what is expected of me. Being real and authentic is perhaps the greatest value of the Millennial generation. But I would argue, the Millennials are not alone. Increasingly, people of every age group are beginning to wrestle with the importance of living honestly—living a life that has integrity, authenticity, and meaning.

How do I live life to its fullest? How do I become the truest me? Is it even possible to *be who I truly am?*

What if our current quest for identity and meaning in our lives can be found in the ancient wisdom of Jesus? What if the whole reason Jesus came to planet Earth was to reveal how we can actually be the best version of ourselves and "live life to the fullest"? (John 10:10b).

I believe the starting point of our search is the realization that we have all been handed lenses that determine how we perceive God, ourselves, and others. These inherited or acquired lenses also greatly affect the way we read the Bible.

Seeing through correct lenses opens our imagination to see our truest identity in Christ and just how vast and inclusive God's Kingdom actually is. Unfortunately, most of us have been handed lenses that are either scratched with denominational preferences or worse yet, damaged by religious tradition, racial prejudice, and national pride that supersedes the message of the Kingdom of God. I want to give a synopsis of six types of corrective lenses that I believe are vital to seeing God, the Bible, ourselves, and others clearly. These lenses are primary for *making sense of the Bible* and *having a vision of who I truly am.*[2]

> We have all been handed lenses that determine how we read the Bible and perceive God, ourselves and others.

- 🔍 A Realigned Lens
- 🔍 A Jesus Lens
- 🔍 A Goodness-of-God Lens
- 🔍 A Covenant and Kingdom Lens
- 🔍 A Better Covenant Lens
- 🔍 An Advancing Kingdom Lens

REALIGNED LENS

Perhaps the greatest hindrance to experiencing God in a new and fresh way is our inability to look at things differently. We become captives to our past teaching and experiences (or lack of experiences).

Perhaps the greatest hindrance to experiencing God in a new and fresh way is our inability to look at things differently. We become captives to our past teaching and experiences (or lack of experiences).

I wonder if Peter, while penning *"God opposes the proud, but gives grace to the humble,"* is reflecting back on his own encounter with God that occurred many years earlier. In Acts 10 we read about Peter's moment of "repentance" that occurs after his verbal wrestling match with God. Peter has to change his entire way of thinking in order to align with God's perspective.

Having grown up a good Jewish boy, Peter understands the etiquette of his day. No self-respecting Jew would ever invite a Gentile into his home, let alone share a meal or travel to meet inside the home of a Gentile. But God has a new plan for Peter—a plan that He has had for all eternity. God is introducing Peter to His Better Covenant that is welcoming of all.

In Acts 10:13-16, God uniquely and supernaturally reveals Himself to Peter. Notice, God meets Peter where he is. God knows all of our prejudices, traditional entrapments, and fears. So, He uses a trance and a strange vision to get Peter's attention. It seems God usually needs to bypass our minds to change our hearts.

Sometimes our religion and tradition get in the way of the new revelation the Holy Spirit is trying to unveil to us. And like Peter, we find ourselves arguing with God. Our heavenly Father is calling us to repent (*metanoia*), but we are so convinced of our way that we miss God's New Covenant way completely.

As I read of Peter's argument with God in Acts 10:9-16, I find myself wondering, will Peter "get it"? Will he embrace this new revelation of the Gospel's inclusivity and availability for *all* to experience the love of the Father, Jesus, and Holy Spirit? Will he be able to overcome his strong ethnic, national pride and unbending racial prejudice? Will his Old Covenant mindset and religious tradition, passed down for more than 1,400 years, block God's new way?

Will Peter stay in his safe, comfortable, acceptable way of doing things? Or, will Peter step into God's assignment and become a world changer?

The truth is, if Peter accepts his mission, everything will change! So, Peter is literally wrestling "in his mind" with God. God is requiring Peter to repent, to align his way of thinking with His. Peter, on the other hand, is "wanting God to repent" and align to Peter's way of thinking—to keep the old ways intact. Have you ever thought of it that way?

Repentance (Greek: *metanoia*) is a "good" word. Seeing clearly with a **realigned lens,** a God-lens, must be our endgame. We must be willing to change our way of thinking over and over again in order to move forward in our relationship with God and His mission. With each new revelation of the Holy Spirit comes *metanoia*

> Repentance is a good word! It means "to change your way of thinking to align with God's perspective."

repentance. We can't stay the way we are and move on with God!

Peter's repentance literally advanced the Kingdom of God forward and opened a way for all peoples to enter. Peter's repentance was culture-transforming. His courage to change, changed the world!

JESUS LENS

One of my favorite stories in the Bible is found in Luke 24:13-35. It's the story of the two disciples of Jesus on the road to Emmaus on the evening of the resurrection. Verse 27 in *The Passion Translation* says, *"Then he (Jesus) carefully unveiled to them the revelation of himself throughout the Scripture. He started from the beginning and explained the writings of Moses and all the prophets, showing how they wrote of him and revealed the truth about himself."* Jesus is declaring that He is the fulfillment of everything that Scripture is. He is the Word made flesh!

> Once you see Jesus unveiled in the Old Testament, everything changes.

Verses 31-32 (TPT) declare, *"All at once their eyes were opened and they realized it was Jesus! Then suddenly, in a flash, Jesus vanished from before their eyes! Stunned, they looked at each other and said, 'Why didn't we recognize it was him? Didn't our hearts burn with the flames of holy passion while we walked beside him? He unveiled for us such profound revelation from the Scriptures!'"*

Jesus' revelation is that He is the culmination of Scripture. He is the final and fullest revelation of God—He is the living Word of God.

Once you finally see Jesus unveiled in the (Old Testament) Scriptures, everything changes. Once you see Jesus revealed as the Word made flesh, everything shifts. And once you see that Jesus is the culmination and resolution of the Old Covenant, you'll never read the Bible the same! You'll begin to see types and shadows of Jesus in virtually every book of the Old Testament. Perhaps for the first time in your life you will be able to make sense of the Bible.

Greater yet, *you* will never be the same! Now you are reading and living as Jesus prescribed—through a **Jesus Lens.** Now you're seeing Jesus as He truly is—the fullest revelation of God the Father and Scripture.

The passage that helped me see that the Jesus Lens provides the key to understanding Scripture is John 5. Jesus wraps up His conversation with the incensed Jewish leaders by firing this shot at impotent religion: *"You study the Scriptures diligently because you think that in them you have eternal life. These are the very*

Scriptures that testify about me (Jesus), yet you refuse to come to me to have life" (John 5:39-40, with parentheses mine).

Jesus is saying that the only way to truly make sense of the Scriptures is to read them with a Jesus Lens, because the Scriptures testify about Him. In *Sinners in the Hands of a Loving God*, Brian Zahnd writes:

> The Scriptures are a means to an end, but not the end itself. If we see the Bible as an end in itself instead of an inspiring witness pointing to Jesus, it will become an idol . . . If we want to make the Bible our final authority, which is an act of idolatry, we are conveniently ignoring the problem that we can make the Bible say just about whatever we want . . . the historical examples are nearly endless: crusaders, slaveholders, and Nazis have all proved their ideologies with images drawn from the Bible. Therefore, we must see the Bible as the penultimate word of God that points us to the ultimate Word of God, who is Jesus. Jesus followers should think of Jesus first and the Bible second.[3]

We all have lenses through which we see life, God, and Scripture. The most effective way to "look" at the Bible is through the Jesus Lens. He is the living Word of God who makes sense of the Bible. (See John 1:14.)

PROGRESSIVE REVELATION
Historical Context

Today, many see the Old Testament as primitive and outdated. It's full of violence, bloody genocide, abuses against human rights, and killing in the name of an angry God. Unfortunately, pastors often give really weak explanations and excuses for God's bad behavior. It's an awkward dance, even for those like myself who love the Bible and believe in its inspiration.

In order for Scripture to become relevant to non-religious, thinking people in the twenty-first century, something must change! I believe that change is the reading of the Bible through a Jesus Lens.

First, we must admit that the Bible, in its writings and content, is wonderfully complex. We do not do it justice —nor are we able to discern God's will—by simply gathering a handful of verses from various books of the Bible and coming up with an interpretation. If we did, we'd still be embracing slavery, polygamy, and concubinage.

Second, a systematic theology that pieces verses together around particular themes found throughout the Bible may have some value, but if this topical approach is divorced from the actual larger story the Bible is trying to convey, it will be confusing at best.

Third, it's imperative that we apply a historical context lens to the progression of the Grand Story in order for the story to make sense. Using a historical contextual interpretation makes it possible to understand what was going on (behind the scenes) during that time period and easier to grasp the intent of what the author is communicating to his original audience. A historical context lens helps us see God's progressive revelation toward a preferred future in even the most primitive Old Testament stories.

In applying the Jesus Lens, two concepts are vital: *divine accommodation* and *progressive revelation*. *Divine accommodation* simply means that God meets people where they are, not where He wishes they were. Why? Because He is a loving Father. His love is patient and kind. He is not easily angered but rather quick to forgive. He rejoices when we discover the truth. Our heavenly Father always protects, always trusts, always hopes, always perseveres. Our Father's love for us never fails (1 Corinthians 13:4-8). Aren't you glad? I know I am.

> **Divine accommodation means that God meets people where they are, not where He wishes they were.**

Most parents understand this principle in raising children through the various stages of maturity. For instance,

Moses' writings (Exodus, Leviticus, Numbers, and Deuteronomy) were given to Israel when she was very immature. She had come out of 400+ years of slavery and its accompanying slave-mindedness. The next 1,400 years would be long, hard years before the coming of Jesus the Messiah and the New Covenant, which would bring a whole new way of thinking and living.

Progressive revelation means that God did not unfold His entire plan to humanity in the Old Testament. The Old Testament revelation, though accurate, is incomplete. The fullness of certain teachings cannot be found in the Old Testament alone. For instance, in the New Testament letter *Ephesians,* Paul writes:

> *"There has never been a generation that has been given the detailed understanding of this glorious and divine mystery until now. He kept it a secret until this generation. God is revealing it now to his sacred apostles and prophets by the Holy Spirit"* (Ephesian 3:5 TPT).

Simply stated, the Bible is progressive in its revelation because God meets people where they are in their ability to comprehend His ways.

If one reads the Bible in a "flat" manner, it will seem contradictory. Brian Zahnd insightfully writes, "The Old Testament Scriptures themselves are on a journey to discover Jesus. They don't stand above the story they tell but are rather enmeshed in it."[4]

GOODNESS-OF-GOD LENS

God's revelation has continually unfolded in stages as we humans were ready to receive it. The ultimate revelation of God is found in Jesus Christ!

> *In the past God spoke to our ancestors through the prophets at many times and in various ways, but in these last days he has spoken to us by His Son whom he appointed heir of all things, and through whom also he made the universe. The Son is the radiance of God's glory and exact representation of his being . . .* (Hebrews 1:1-3 NIV).

Since Jesus is the exact representation of God, His view of God and His nature and ways are the most intimate, accurate, and full representation available. In fact, Jesus and the Father are one. Jesus IS God (John 1:1-5, 14-18)!

So how did Jesus portray His Father?

In Luke 15, Jesus tells a story that illustrates the **goodness** of God as our loving Father. It presents the **Goodness-of-God Lens** that is necessary to understand God and His ways.

Jesus is communicating to two different audiences: first, ". . . tax collectors and sinners who had gathered to hear Jesus" (v.1), and second, "the Pharisees and teachers of the law who were muttering in the background, 'This man welcomes sinners and eats with them'" (v.2).

What a great setting for Jesus to illustrate what the Father heart of God is truly like. The tax collectors and sinners represent the outcasts of society. They were considered irreligious and unacceptable to God. The Pharisees and teachers of the law represent the religious experts, the spiritually elite who were "in the know."

Jesus goes straight to His main point in Luke 15:11-32. Hang on, Pharisees and teachers of the Law, Jesus is about to blow your minds and sink your ship—which is carrying 1,400 years of theology. He is going to tell a story that will let you—and the rest of society—know once and for all what God is really like! He's going to challenge the hierarchy of religion and level the playing field—through grace. Take notice: God is nothing like the record-keeping, law-wielding judge that you have imagined. No! He's a loving, generous, forgiving Father.

For years, Jesus had been continuously referring to God as "Father" as He journeyed through Judea. Clearly, the father in this story represents God; thus, when referring to the dad in the story, I will capitalize the noun Father.

The first thing we notice about the Father's goodness is that **He doesn't manipulate or control us**, but gives us a choice, even to make the wrong choice. True relationship demands that we have the ability to choose.

In this case, the younger son chooses to exercise absolute self-centeredness. He knows what he wants and is determined to get it. Requesting his inheritance early is tantamount to him saying, "Old man, I wish You were dead. I want to take from You so I can do what I want. I want to be free and independent of You and get as far away from Your sight as possible!" This is

> **The Father's goodness doesn't manipulate or control us.**

our modern-day definition of what it means to be prodigal. So, the younger son collects his inheritance and heads for the far country, far away from his Father (Luke 15:11-19).

In Luke 15:20-24, we see the Father's response to His disrespectful, prodigal son, who by now has squandered his entire inheritance on shameful living and is returning home, smelling like pig slop and filled with shame, guilt, fear, and disgrace.

Take note, even the stench of pigpen living cannot stop the Father's goodness and love toward His son. **The Father's love is filled with compassion,** for He runs to His son, throws His arms around him, kisses him, clothes him, and honors him before the entire community with an extravagant feast and celebration!

In Luke 15:22-24 (NIV), we read:

> But the father said to his servants, "Quick! Bring the best robe and put it on him. Put a ring on his finger and sandals on his feet. Bring the fattened calf and kill it. Let's have a feast and celebrate. For this son of mine was dead and is alive again; he was lost and is found." So they began to celebrate.

The Father's love is a covenant love. It calls out our true identity and gives us the very best.

Luke 15:25-32 (NIV) records the perspective of the older son, who has been working in the fields and is just returning home for the evening. When he hears music and sees dancing, he asks a servant what is going on. "Your kid brother is home, and your dad has thrown a huge party to celebrate his safe return."

The older son gets so angry that he refuses to join the celebration. Interestingly, in Near Eastern culture, the oldest son's role would have been to help host and entertain the guests at such an event. So, the elder son is both angry and disobedient.

> . . . So, his father went out and pleaded with him. But he answered his father, "Look! All these years I've been slaving for you and never disobeyed your orders. Yet you never gave me even a young goat so I could celebrate with my friends. But

when this son of yours who has squandered your property with prostitutes comes home, you kill the fattened calf for him!"

"My son," the father said, "you are always with me, and everything I have is yours. But we had to celebrate and be glad, because this brother of yours was dead and is alive again; he was lost and is found."

The Father's love pleads for true harmony in His family. Again, we see the Father disregarding the social norm of the day, which demanded honor for the father of a household. No socially conscious father would have gone outside to *plead* with his disobedient, older son.

> The Father's love can only be offered, it cannot be imposed.

However, this Father takes the road of dishonor and even shame in hopes of restoring relationship with His elder son and harmony between the two sons.

Notice how the Father appeals to his son's spirit and not to his mind. To the natural man, this seems like foolishness or weakness, but in reality, it reveals that **the Father's love can only be offered and it cannot be imposed.**

THE TRUTH

You cannot be bad enough to make the Father quit loving you, and you cannot be good enough to make the Father love you more! He's simply a good, good Father who desires to see you free and whole—living out your truest identity!

THE POINT

Jesus came from heaven to earth to **reveal** what the goodness of our Father is like, and to **restore** us back to relationship with Himself and His Father in the power of the Holy Spirit (John 17:3,20-23).

THE QUESTION

Will you repent (align with Father's perspective) and trust in Jesus and His salvation? (Mark 1:15).

COVENANT AND KINGDOM LENS

The two primary themes that thread through the Bible are *Covenant* and *Kingdom.*

Covenant is the way the Bible describes and defines *relationship*; first our relationship with God and then our relationship with everyone else.

The Bible is, in fact, a written record of God's progressive covenant journey with humanity.[5] The word **"covenant"** means *to become one*. God's desire from the beginning was that mankind would live in unfettered union with Him. He desired that, when anyone looked at us, they would see Him (Genesis 1:26-27). Thus, man's true identity is found in oneness with God (John 17).

> **The Bible is a written record of God's progressive covenant journey with humanity.**

Kingdom reveals our God-given *responsibility* and authority as His representatives on earth (Genesis 1:26-28). Kingdom follows covenant because responsibility always follows relationship. Mankind's fundamental responsibility was and still is *to re-present God.* As God's representatives, *"The Lord God took the man and put him in the Garden of Eden to work it and take care of it"* (Genesis 2:15 NIV).

Our task today is still quite simple—to oversee and care for all creation (starting with our fellow man) and to advance the Kingdom of God on planet Earth.

BETTER COVENANT LENS

Today, on this side of the cross, we enjoy all the New Covenant benefits of Jesus' resurrection, ascension, enthronement, and outpouring of His Holy Spirit. As Spirit-indwelled believers, we are forgiven—once-for-all, and now have the Holy Spirit living inside of us. Paul anticipated that perhaps the greatest issue for born-again believers would be that they would not know "who they are" and "who lives within them." For this reason, he wrote:

> **Everything changed at the Cross!**

> Do you not know that your bodies are temples of the Holy Spirit, who is in you, whom you have received from God? You are not your own; you were bought at a price. Therefore, honor God with your bodies (1 Corinthians 6:19-20 NIV).

Paul was declaring that **everything changed at the cross**. A New Covenant had been inaugurated by Jesus, and now the Father and Jesus were both available to all through the Holy Spirit. But Paul didn't stop there. He asserted that our bodies are the dwelling place of the Holy Spirit, and we can experience true fellowship and oneness with God in Christ by the power of the Holy Spirit.

Let that sink in. It's scandalous! It's total restoration to God's intended purpose for mankind. I am one with God in Christ by the power of the Holy Spirit who lives in me! And it's all because of The Cross Event. On this side of the Cross . . .

- We are no longer servants (Old Covenant mentality), but friends of Jesus (*John 15:15*).

- We are no longer slaves of fear (Old Covenant mentality), but adopted sons and co-heirs with Christ (*Romans 8:15-17*).

- We live loved because we live in God and God lives in us. God's perfect love drives out all fear *(1 John 4:16-18*).

- We no longer need to make continual sacrifices; Jesus is our once-for-all sacrifice for the forgiveness of sin (*Hebrews 7:27*).

- We are no longer sin-conscious; we are now righteousness-conscious (*2 Corinthians 5:17, 21*).

- We no longer strive to obey 613 laws of the Old Covenant; we now live by one law, the law of love (*John 13:34-35*).

The New Covenant transformed discipleship from *imitating a mentor* into *cultivating fellowship with the resurrected Jesus Christ* living within you and then *emanating Him* wherever you go (*Colossians 1:27*).

The writer of Hebrews understood the revelation of a New and Better Covenant:

> *Because God gave His word, Jesus makes certain the promise of a **better covenant** (Hebrews 7:22 NIRV—emphasis mine).*

> *. . . The days are coming, declares the Lord, when I will make a **new covenant** . . . It will not be like the covenant I made with their ancestors . . . By calling this covenant **'new,'** He has made the first one obsolete; and what is obsolete and outdated will soon disappear (Hebrews 8:8-9,13 NIV—emphasis mine).*

ADVANCING KINGDOM LENS

Years ago, I heard a talk about the Kingdom of God by Myles Munroe that was transformational. Through the years, this seminal message has expanded into my own thoughts and theology, but the general points are the same. **The Bible is about . . .**

A King. A sovereign Lord of all. We do not have a vote.

A Royal Family. We are sons and daughters of the most high King. We are royalty. God is King of kings, not King of subjects!

A Kingdom. The King's domain includes everything that is owned by the King. The King's dominion is the King's rule and reign over all.

A Colonization Project. God's purpose is not to get us to heaven, but rather God sent man to earth to colonize earth for heaven—to extend and expand the King's influence.

The Colony of Earth's "Declaration of Independence." Earth's first man, Adam/Eve, disobeyed God and cut off their heavenly governor—the Holy Spirit (*Genesis 2:7*).

The Devastation of Mankind's "Declaration of Independence." Unfortunately, the bulk of the Bible (Old Testament) records the journey of a desperately "lost" people. This sheer volume can often veil the ecstasy of the Good News of . . .

The Redemption and Restoration of Humanity through Jesus Christ. This is the Good News, to which everything in the Bible points!

The Advancement of the Kingdom of God through Spirit-filled humanity. This advancing of God's Kingdom on earth has been unfolding since the incarnation of God in the birth of Jesus. During His ministry, Jesus' central message was "the kingdom of God is in your midst, so change your way of thinking and start believing the unbelievable good news" (*Mark 1:15*).

This Good News of the Kingdom is our good news to both embrace and share with others. Because the Kingdom of God was manifested fully in Jesus' life, death, resurrection, and current enthronement as King of kings, we are now partakers of His forgiveness, new life, and ambassadorial authority. Because the Holy Spirit was poured out at Pentecost, we are empowered to do the works of Jesus on earth as it is in heaven.

> The Good News of the Kingdom is our good news to both embrace and share with others.

 **GRACE REFLECTIONS**
Journaling My Thoughts

1. Why is repentance (metanoia) a good word?

LIVING LOVED

2. Think back on a time you argued with or questioned God and His ways. Did this result in you hardening your heart in anger and frustration, or did it cause you to have a transformational rethink of your ideas? Explain.

3. Is reading the Bible through a Jesus Lens a different paradigm for you? How were you challenged or encouraged with the idea of progressive revelation?

42

4. Why is seeing God as a good and loving Father so important?

5. What does "living on the right side of the cross" mean to you?

6. How might an Advancing Kingdom Lens affect your view of current and end time events?

03
MAKING DISCIPLES OF JESUS IS NORMAL
Living Loved, Living Full, Living Free

There is a lot of talk in Christian circles about "revival." Well, what is meant when one says, "What we really need is revival"? Each denomination or non-denomination has its own definition. Perhaps what we really need is a return to "normal." But **what is normal?**

In order to answer that question, we must first distinguish between *average* and *normal*. In *Normal Christianity,* Jonathan Welton points out an important truth:

> Most Christians process their lives through **averages,** comparing their spirituality against the backdrop of neighbors, friends, their church family members, and relatives . . . "My church has great worship (or preaching) compared to the church I used to attend." Normal is a completely different measurement. **Normal is based on comparing with an ideal**. Abnormal means that there is an aberration from the standard of what is considered

normal. Jesus is the example of *normal* for the Christian. To be different from Jesus in any way is to be an aberration from the standard set by His life.[6]

When I was 24 years old, my seminary professor stepped to the lectern during a class in which we were studying the book of *Acts* and boldly declared, "The narrative of the early church is not normative for Christian living today!"

In an automatic reflex, I found myself raising my hand and asking, "Can you help me understand why *Acts* is not normative for today?" He responded, "Because we are no longer experiencing the great exploits of the early Church . . . we now have the Bible as our guide for faith and living." That answer didn't satisfy me then and is still unacceptable today.

> **NORMAL is what Jesus says and does in and through His disciples.**

Average, what most are experiencing (or not experiencing), is not the standard! We must not compare ourselves with others to determine normative Christian living. **Normal is the Jesus way. Normal is what Jesus says and does in and through His disciples. Jesus described normal like this:**

You will receive power when the Holy Spirit comes on you; and you will be my witnesses . . . (Acts 1:8 NIV).

I tell you the truth, anyone who believes in me will do the same works I have done, and even greater works, because I am going to the Father (John 14:12 NLT).

. . . 'As the Father has sent Me, I am sending you.' And with that Jesus breathed on them and said, 'Receive the Holy Spirit' (John 20:21-22 NIV).

And these signs will accompany those who believe: In my name they will drive out demons; they will speak with new tongues . . . they will place their hands on sick people, and they will get well (Mark 16:17 NIV).

The Apostle John went so far as to say:

*"Whoever claims to live in him (Jesus) **must live as Jesus did**"* (1 John 2:6 NIV—emphasis mine).

The primary purpose of this book is to help you be a normal disciple and disciple-maker. Let's return to normal![7]

WHAT IS A DISCIPLE OF JESUS?

ALL wholehearted followers of Jesus are disciples of Jesus. On the right side of the cross, we no longer view Jesus as our great human rabbi (2 Corinthians 5:16).

Jesus is now our Savior and King. There are two vital aspects of being a Better Covenant disciple:

- **Being** who I truly am as a *new creation in Christ* (2 Corinthians 5:17, 21).

- **Re-presenting** my King as *His ambassador on earth* (2 Corinthians 5:20).

These two functions describe the life of grace. Here's a good definition of grace:

> Grace is God's empowering presence that enables me to **be** who He created me to be and to **re-present** what He is truly like.

BEING describes *my life in Christ* (2 Corinthians 5:17). As a New Covenant disciple of Jesus, I grow by cultivating an abiding relationship with the resurrected Jesus Christ who lives inside of me. My being is *my identity* that flows from *my union in Christ.* It's who I truly am—a human being! My purpose as a human being is to *live loved* and *live free* in Christ!

RE-PRESENTING describes *Christ's life in me* (Colossians 1:27). As a Kingdom representative of Jesus, I emanate His life and re-present His authority everywhere I go! My *union in Christ* is the source of my

> **BEING describes my life in Christ. RE-PRESENTING describes Christ's life in me.**

purity and *power* in God. It's vital to understand that all of my holiness (purity) flows from the *Holy* Spirit who lives within me (1 Corinthians 6:19-20). In the same way, all of my authority and power flows from my Father's endorsement (2 Corinthians 5:20), and the Spirit living inside me. My purpose as an ambassador of Christ is to *live free* and *live full* in Christ!

Jesus summarized the life of a New Covenant disciple this way:

> *I am the vine; you are the branches. If you remain (abide) in Me and I in you, you will bear much fruit; apart from Me you can do nothing* (John 15:5 NIV—parenthesis mine).

I remind you, fruit is the "excess life" of Jesus flowing through us because we are in union with and indwelled by Him. What others see as the fruit of your labor, Jesus sees as the overflow of His life gushing from yours. That's guilt-free, striving-free, Better Covenant discipleship. Or as Paul called it—life *in* Christ.

In short, a New Covenant disciple is one who has learned how to live loved, live full, and live free! The fruit (excess life) of the Spirit flows out of his or her union with Christ.

HOW DO I MAKE DISCIPLES OF JESUS?

The process of making disciples is simpler than you imagine. In fact, I would argue that disciple-making is fairly instinctive for heathy "abiding" disciples of Jesus.

Here are a few tips:

Show up. It's very difficult to make disciples from a distance. Disciple-making at its core is *life-on-life*. It's intentionally showing you care and that individuals matter.

Be present. Active listening shows honor and respect. The old saying is true, *"People don't care how much you know until they know how much you care."*

In his discipleship training, my friend Murray Newman says, "People are asking three questions:

1. **Do you know me?** People *belong* because they are known and loved. People *believe* because they belong. People *become* because of what they believe.

2. **Do you understand me?** Have you listened to me enough to know why I do what I do?

3. **Can you help me?** Do you have the wisdom and resources that can meet my needs and help me grow up?"

Remind people who they are. Remind them of their *identity* and *union in Christ*. Help them *cultivate sensitivity to the indwelling Holy Spirit.* Chapters 5-19 are designed to assist you in helping others understand who they truly are in Christ.

Process life together. Share life together. What is working? What is not working? This usually happens naturally in the flow of conversation. Remember, our secret weapon is the Holy One who lives inside of us, enabling us to live pure and powerful lives. Much of *processing life together* is simply asking each other the right clarifying questions, and then trusting the Spirit to give wisdom and direction.

Offer both Invitation and Challenge. *Invitation* is about welcoming someone into a *relationship* that allows them access to your life. *Challenge* confronts behaviors that are either wrong, unhealthy, or need adjustment. It provides the opportunity to accept the *responsibilities* of discipleship.[8]

Consider these reflections on my *Experiencing God* group, from Chapter 1:

This group was a parenthesis in our busy weeks, where we could let our hair down and freely share our honest feelings, dreams, hurts, and struggles without fear of shame or judgment. Our EG group was a "safe place" where we could receive care, comfort, and support. It was a place where vulnerability was not only encouraged but applauded. It was a place of both **invitation and challenge!** I think the phrase *mutual encouragement* best describes what this group offered me. We all need to be told, "You can do this; you have what it takes!" Encouragement means *"to give courage."* We all need a safe place to give and receive courage. We all need a safe place to give and receive support, confidence, and hope.

Former Wheaton College football coach Mike Swider has said, "Influence occurs and relationships are built around four things: *inspiring* and *encouraging* people and *confronting* and *challenging* people. As a coach or mentor, 70–80% of your discussions with others ought to be *encouraging* and *inspiring*. While 20–30% of your discussions ought to be *challenging and confronting!*" This mix of invitation and challenge will result in deep and fruitful relationships because this is the makeup of all healthy relationships.[9]

DISCIPLE-MAKING IS AS SIMPLE AS BEING FAMILY

*I remind you, dear **children**: your sins have been permanently removed because of the power of his name. I remind you, **fathers and mothers**: you have a relationship with the One who has existed from the beginning. I remind you, **young people**: you <u>have</u> defeated the Evil One* (1 John 2:12-13 TPT).

What if we viewed the family of God as just that—a family? What if *being a disciple* is as simple as being who I truly am as a new creation in Christ, with the help of spiritual *fathers and mothers* who can share their wisdom and *brothers and sisters* who are fellow learners on the journey of life? What if *making disciples* is as simple as "re-presenting" what God is truly like in the season of life I am living? (1 John 2:12-14). What if better covenant discipleship is actually about being a **family on mission**?

> **INVITATION** is about welcoming someone into a relationship that allows them access to your life.

Notice the three seasons of maturity John mentions: *fathers and mothers, children,* and *young people.* Larry Kreider shares the following wisdom regarding spiritual family:

Fathers and mothers. Spiritual parenting is a behind-the-scenes venture. There are not many "pats on the back." But the reality is—being a parent is not something you *do* as much as it is who you *are.* The measure of the greatness of a spiritual parent is always the measure of servanthood and love.

What do parents do for their children?

- Parents love and encourage their children. They help their spiritual son or daughter reach his or her God-given potential.

- Parents give children a sense of significance by providing protection and security, teaching them their true identity and union in Christ, and empowering them to re-present Christ in the unique way He has called them.

- Parents expect their children to grow up into mature adults (this is the endgame).

- Parents set an example for their children. They model what healthy parenting looks like.

- A parent's goal is to raise up spiritually heathy sons and daughters who can do the same . . . (this endgame will never be accomplished if parents coddle their kids into co-dependency, thereby stunting their ability to "launch" and start a family of their own).

Growing from a spiritual baby into a spiritual parent is crucial to God's divine order. That's why God established "growth stages" through which we grow to parenthood.

Children. Spiritual babies in the Body of Christ are wonderful. Any good spiritual parent is happy to spend extra time with them in order to steer them in the right direction. 1 John 2:12 helps us understand that parenting new believers primarily consists of helping them understand their new identity in Christ and that they are forever forgiven because of the once-for-all sacrifice of Jesus (Hebrews 7:27; 8:12; 9:26-28).

A new believer often acts like a natural child—self-centered, immature, gullible, and unstable. Spiritual babies, just like natural babies, may need to be spoon-fed for a season. In time, with care, love, and understanding of their new identity in Christ and His indwelling Spirit, they will move into the next stage of growth.

Young people. Young men and women have learned how to feed themselves as they meditate on the Word of God. According to 1 John 2:14, young people are strong with God's Word in their hearts. They have learned how

CHALLENGE confronts behaviors that are wrong, unhealthy or need adjustment.

to apply God's Word, both the written Word (Bible), the living Word (Jesus) and the prophetic Word (from the Spirit of God). They don't need to run to others to care for them like babies do because they have learned how to apply the Word to their own lives.

One particularly important aspect of young men and women is that they not only know their identity in Christ, but they also know their authority in Christ. They confidently enter into spiritual battles knowing that they fight *from* a place of victory (the cross and resurrection), not *for* victory. This is a huge difference-maker in daily living![10]

WHY MAKE DISCIPLES?

Jesus said to "make disciples of all nations . . ." (Matthew 28:19-20). Plain and simple, Spirit led disciple-making is Jesus' method to "change the world"!

Our investment in people matters. Lives are transformed one-at-a-time! Our presence and engagement in the lives of others matters. Many people flow in and out of our lives during various seasons, but whether we realize it or not, our influence on others is much greater than we imagine.

Recently, after giving a talk at a *Men's Walk to Emmaus* weekend, a man whom I had never met named Danny came up to me and said, "I've been wrestling with a call into vocational ministry, and some of the things you shared in your talk spoke to me. Would you mind sharing the story of your call to ministry with me?"

I shared, "Well, my story is pretty uneventful. When I was 20 years old, I began working with a small church in New Braunfels, Texas, which has since become one of the largest churches in that city . . ."

Danny interrupted me, "Was that church Oakwood Baptist Church?"

I nodded quizzically.

"What year was that?" Danny inquired.

"1982," I answered.

Danny smiled and continued, "Do you know Rick K., Bryan R., Robin R., and Melissa P.?"

Stunned, I replied, "Sure, they were all in my first youth group."

Filled with emotion, Danny said, "I was in your youth group . . . thirty-seven years ago. I was the younger brother of Melissa."

Then almost as if time had been turned back, Danny looked at me and asked, "Would you be willing to disciple me?"

Our investment in others matters, whether we realize it or not. Lives are transformed life-on-life . . . one-at-a-time . . . in due season!

WHAT DOES DISCIPLE-MAKING LOOK LIKE ON THIS SIDE OF THE CROSS?

I am often asked, "Is disciple-making today the same as it was when Jesus walked the earth and made disciples of the original twelve?" For years, my answer would have been an emphatic, "Absolutely, Jesus is our model for disciple-making, and His method is our blueprint!"

And while I still believe making disciples of all nations is our mandate from Jesus, I no longer believe that we make disciples in the same way Jesus initially did. *Why*, you ask? Well, because on the right side of the cross, we

> On the right side of the Cross we enjoy all the benefits of Jesus' resurrection, ascension, enthronement and Spirit.

enjoy all the New Covenant benefits of Jesus' resurrection, ascension, enthronement, and outpouring of His Holy Spirit at the birth of His Church at Pentecost. As born-again believers, we now have the Holy Spirit living inside of us.

Jesus actually gave us two strong *hints* of how He saw disciple-making on the right side of the cross. In His Great Commission, He said . . .

> *All authority in heaven and on earth has been given to me. Therefore go and make disciples of all nations . . . And **surely I am with you always, to the very end of the age*** (Matthew 28:19-20 NIV—emphasis mine).

> *On that day you will realize that **I am in my Father, and you are in me, and I am in you*** (John 14:20 NIV—emphasis mine).

In both of the previous verses, Jesus is saying that He will be **with** us, and even more astounding, **in** us, living His life through us by His Spirit.

In essence, disciple-making on the right side of the cross is a family venture that empowers sons and daughters of our loving heavenly Father to live loved, live full and live free.

In the next chapter we will explore the Apostle Paul's discovery of how to make disciples of Jesus while he was in Ephesus. We'll also see why his letter to the Ephesians is a perfect blueprint to help us in both being and making new covenant disciples today.

GRACE REFLECTIONS
Journaling My Thoughts

1. Reflect on Jesus' description of a *normal disciple* in the passages on pages 46 and 47. Are you a normal disciple? Ask God to show you two or three ways you need to shift your thinking. Take time to journal your reflections.

2. Why is *processing life with someone* so important? Who currently helps you process life?

3. Describe how someone has invested in your life in a meaningful way. Was that relationship with a father/mother figure, young person, or child?

4. Describe your relationship with someone with whom you helped process life in a meaningful way.

5. What is the difference between Old Covenant and New Covenant discipleship?

04
A BLUEPRINT FOR BETTER COVENANT DISCIPLESHIP
Paul's Letter to the Ephesians

While I was studying in preparation for the *Normal* series in the book of *Acts*, I began to see the pieces of my disciple-making puzzle coming together. Many commentators refer to Luke's second volume as *The Acts of the Holy Spirit* because of the prominent role of the Holy Spirit. Have you ever wondered why the Holy Spirit plays such a central role in *Acts*? I think Luke is showing us how everything changed after the cross, resurrection, and pouring out of the Holy Spirit. As my friend Bruce likes to say, "Turbo-powered disciple-making is normal on this side of the cross!" The indwelling Holy Spirit changed everything (Romans 8:9-11). Today, turbo-powered discipleship is normal discipleship.

> "Turbo-powered disciple-making is normal on this side of this cross!"
>
> —Bruce Karnes

Reading through *Acts*, I noticed that Paul's mission headquarters was Ephesus. This proved to be a vital discovery. In Paul's day, Ephesus was the largest city in Asia Minor. It was the New York City of the ancient world, serving as the epicenter of worship for most of the Greek and Roman gods and goddesses. In fact, the temple of Artemis (Diana) was one of the Seven Wonders of the Ancient World. Ephesus was also the central hub that connected the Eastern world with the Western world. No city in Asia was more famous, populous, or wealthy.

For nearly three years, approximately AD 54–57, Paul had a strong missionary presence in Ephesus and many people became followers of Jesus Christ. The story of how Paul came to the city of Ephesus is quite interesting. Acts 19 fills in many of the details of that story. But perhaps the most important aspect of Paul's time in Ephesus was his two-year investment in training eight apprentices for the work of planting churches.

Though unfamiliar to most of us today, Paul invested in eight men who became his band of brothers. These men literally "turned the world upside down" with the transforming power of the Gospel (Acts 17:6 NKJV).

That's right! These "no-names" were world-changers. Pause a moment to review and remember the names of these risk-taking heroes of the faith. They are more important than you might imagine.

- Titus (from Antioch),
- Timothy (from Lystra),
- Gaius (from Derbe),
- Sopater (from Berea),
- Aristarchus and Secundus (from Thessalonica),
- Tychicus and Trophimus (from Ephesus).

Paul collected these faithful men from various cities on his Gospel tour and trained them at the Hall of Tyrannus in Ephesus (Acts 19:8-10). There, he laid the foundation for the Ephesian church and many future churches to come. In time Ephesus would become an apostolic hub and the epicenter of revival (normal Christianity).

A few years later, while imprisoned in Rome, Paul wrote a letter to the newly started congregations in the Ephesian region. In time, this letter would become a discipleship guide for establishing new believers and laying a firm foundation for churches. This letter is the epistle we now call *Ephesians*.

So, why did I specifically choose *Ephesians* as the template for Better Covenant disciple-making? Surely, there are other New Covenant letters that could be considered. Yes, there are other letters that ooze with Paul's message of Better Covenant living, but *Ephesians* is unique in that it was not written to address any particular error, problem, or heresy of a specific church.

Ephesians is a letter for all people, in all churches, in all generations.

Rather, it was a *circular letter* intended to be read by the church in Ephesus, as well as the other churches that Paul and his band of church planters had started. *Ephesians* is a letter for all people, in all churches, in all generations.

SEVEN MAJOR THEMES OF DISCIPLE-MAKING EMERGE IN EPHESIANS

The first theme is **GRACE** (Ephesians 2:8-9). Everything in the Better Covenant life begins with grace. Everything in the Better Covenant life is sustained by grace. Everything in the Better Covenant life is accomplished by Jesus' finished work of grace.

Everything in the Better Covenant life begins with and is sustained by grace.

As I write, I am reminded of the first and perhaps most powerful prophetic word I received as a 27-year-old more than thirty years ago: "Father is freeing you from the bondage of religious constraint to be a daring deliverer to others who are entrapped and in need of His **marvelous grace**." This is essentially the message God delivered to Paul at his conversion and the same message that Paul passed on to the churches in the region of Ephesus.

The second theme of *Ephesians* is **IDENTITY.** My truest identity is revealed when I come to know and embrace *who God truly is* and *who I am in Christ.* My identity flows through my union in Christ.

Paul's third theme is **UNITY.** New Covenant **unity** declares that all people groups are *included* through Christ's death and resurrection and we are now *one new humanity in Christ* (Ephesians 2:1-3:6). This union is *lived out* through our *oneness in Christ* (Ephesians 4:1-16).

The heart of the Gospel message is that the Father, Jesus, and Spirit have entered into our world and have received us into their life, making it possible for us to be *one with God in Christ by the power of the Holy Spirit.* Our response to this revelation of the Gospel of grace is either repentance and trusting faith or self-centered pride and rejection of this Good News. *Oneness* is the purpose of the New Covenant and the endgame of God's rescue project that the Bible calls salvation!

> **My identity flows through my union in Christ.**

The fourth theme of *Ephesians* is **MYSTERY.** Ephesians 3 unpacks God's hidden battle plan that is now revealed to New Covenant believers. The theme of God's mysterious grace threads through many of Paul's letters.

The fifth theme of *Ephesians* is **PURITY.** Living a pure life begins with right thinking. Wrong thinking leads to wrong living; right thinking leads to right (pure) living. The struggle for purity starts with wrong thinking, which leads to darkened understanding, which creates the perception of "separation from God." This results in the hardening of our hearts, which produces sexual immorality, greed, lying, anger, stealing, unwholesome talk, bitterness, etc. (Ephesians 4:17-5:17).

> Living a pure life begins with right thinking.

The sixth theme of *Ephesians* is **HARMONY.** Paul portrays harmony through the image of the Spirit-filled home. Nothing displays true Kingdom harmony better than a Spirit-led marriage and family.

The seventh theme of *Ephesians* is **AUTHORITY.** Because I belong to Jesus, I have all the right equipment and full authority to stand against the enemy of my soul (mind, will, emotions). Because of the death, resurrection, indwelling Holy Spirit, and forever enthronement of King Jesus—I now stand in a place of victory. The cross is where my victory occurred. The cross is where the enemy's defeat occurred. Therefore, I am no longer fighting *for* victory. I fight *from* victory (Ephesians 6:10-20)!

TRANSFORMING CULTURE

The goal of the Gospel message has always been cultural transformation—by bringing the culture of heaven to earth! *Ephesians* was written with the purpose of transforming the culture of Ephesus and the surrounding region where churches were being planted by Paul and his comrades. Read within its true historical context, *Ephesians* is an *apostolic letter* written by an apostle to a family of Christ followers who, together, are on a mission to transform the world with the Good News of Jesus Christ and His Kingdom.

> The goal of the Gospel message has always been cultural transformation— bringing the culture of heaven to earth!

The Greek word *apostolos* means "sent one." In Paul's day, an apostle was one sent from his own native kingdom and culture into another territory for the purpose of establishing a new culture that would replicate his native kingdom's culture. An apostle in essence is a "culture changer."

Acts of the Apostles, which contains the story of Paul's time in Ephesus, is an account of how normal disciples of the early church transformed culture. Reading through the first few chapters of *Acts*, one gets a sense of what Jesus expected normal New Covenant living to be like. I want you to notice four manifestations that occur continuously in the newborn church that are a normal part of Better Covenant living.

UNIFIED PRAYER

The first thing the disciples did after gathering in an upper room to wait for the promised coming of the Holy Spirit was to pray. This was uncharted territory for them. No one had ever been baptized in the Holy Spirit before, with the promise of being indwelled permanently.

> *They all joined together constantly in prayer, along with the women and Mary the mother of Jesus, and with his brothers . . . a group numbering about a hundred and twenty (Acts 1:14-15 NIV).*

Unified prayer is our partnering with the purposes of the Kingdom! (See Acts 3:1, 6-10 and Acts 4:23-31 for further examples of the dependence on and influence of prayer in the early church.)

Like the early church, we've discovered *unified prayer* is vital to experiencing the "normal" power of the Kingdom of God. In the spring of 2019, several churches in the San Marcos area, where I live, began to intentionally meet for the purpose of initiating *unceasing prayer* in our region. Today, we are increasingly seeing unified prayer take root. Our goal is to see 24/7/365 prayer become a reality in our region!

> **Unified prayer is our partnering with the purposes of the Kingdom.**

A prayer movement is being established through local churches up and down the I-35 corridor from Austin to San Antonio. My pastor friends in Austin, where I previously resided for 23 years, have ignited "a growing prayer movement involving thousands of people and more than 100 churches in one of America's largest and most unchurched cities."[11] Austin has had unified, unceasing prayer in her city since January 1, 2009.

We believe Isaiah 35 is a prophetic declaration for our I-35 *Cover the Corridor* prayer campaign.

> *And a highway will be there; it will be called the Way of Holiness; it will be for those who walk on that Way . . .*
> (Isaiah 35:8a NIV).

> **Three manifestations of unified prayer are supernatural demonstration, bold proclamation and city transformation.**

As a result of following the Way, and our call to emanate His holiness, many churches are now beginning to experience three manifestations of unified prayer that the church of *Acts* experienced: *supernatural demonstration, bold proclamation,* and *city transformation*!

SUPERNATURAL DEMONSTRATION

After ten days of constant prayer while waiting for the coming of the Holy Spirit in life-transforming power, the prayer of those 120 faithful was finally realized:

> *When the day of Pentecost came, they were all together in one place (in Jerusalem, in constant prayer). Suddenly, a sound like the blowing of a violent wind came from heaven and filled the whole house . . . They saw what seemed to be tongues of fire that separated and came to rest on each of them. All were filled with the Holy Spirit and began to speak in other tongues as the Spirit enabled them (Acts 2:1-4 NIV—parenthesis mine).*

Even metaphorically, when your head catches on fire and your tongue is sanctified with a new language, that qualifies as a supernatural demonstration. (See Acts 3:6-10 and Acts 4:13-20 for further examples of the supernatural demonstration of *normal* Christianity.)

BOLD PROCLAMATION

The coming of the Holy Spirit in power has corresponding purpose and responsibility. But, as you might guess, the onlooking crowd had various opinions:

> When they heard this sound, a crowd came together in bewilderment, because each one heard their own language being spoken. Utterly amazed, they asked: Aren't all these who are speaking Galileans? (They don't speak my language) . . . Amazed and perplexed, they asked one another, "What does this mean?" Some, however, made fun of them and said, "They have had too much wine" (Acts 2:6-7, 12-13 NIV—parenthesis mine).

This was the perfect setup for Peter's bold proclamation of the Gospel message:

> These people are not drunk, as you suppose. It's only nine in the morning! No, this (what you have experienced today) is what was spoken by the prophet Joel: "In the last days, God says, I will pour out my Spirit on all people. Your sons and daughters will prophesy, your young men will see visions, your old men will dream dreams . . . everyone who calls upon the name of the Lord will be saved" (Acts 2:15-21 NIV—parenthesis mine).

CITY TRANSFORMATION

The result of Peter's Pentecost message is found in Acts 2:37-38, 41(NIV):

> When the people heard this message, they were cut to the heart and said to Peter and the other apostles, "Brothers, what shall we do?" Peter replied, "Repent and be baptized, every one of you, in the name of Jesus Christ for the forgiveness of your sins. And you will receive the gift of the Holy Spirit..." Those who accepted his message were baptized, and about three thousand were added to their number that day.

In time, this group of spiritual revolutionaries would be known as those who turned the world upside-down with the message of Jesus and the Kingdom of God. (See Acts 4:1-20 and Acts 5:12-42 for further examples of city transformation through the power of the Gospel of the Kingdom and New Covenant.)

Tragically, today what we call "revival" is actually what Jesus expected the new *normal* of Christ-following to look like. We are New Covenant ambassadors of the Kingdom of God, the manifestation of God's ruling presence.

So, is the Kingdom advancing today?

Contrary to what doomsday prophets and pessimistic defeatists say, the Church is not being defeated. She is not at the mercy of the devil or fallen society. The truth is, the Kingdom of heaven is expanding, advancing, and growing like never before in the history of mankind. We simply need a better lens to see what our Father is up to. [12]

Followers of Jesus are to be culture changers, advancing the Kingdom of God everywhere we are and everywhere we go! The culture we carry is that of a New and Better Covenant (Hebrews 8:13).

 **GRACE REFLECTIONS**
Journaling My Thoughts

1. How are you currently experiencing God's empowering presence?

2. What does abiding trust and union with Christ look like to you?

3. How might you view each mystery as an invitation to greater intimacy?

4. How would you live differently if you understood that your purity (holiness) comes from the Holy Spirit who lives in you?

5. How will you live as an ambassador of Jesus, commissioned to be a **culture changer**?

Part II
LIVING LOVED

Living Loved describes *my life* in Christ (2 Corinthians 5:17). As a New Covenant disciple of Jesus, I grow by cultivating an abiding relationship with the resurrected Jesus Christ, who lives inside of me. My being must always precede my doing. Why? Because *my true identity* flows from *my union in Christ*. It's who I truly am —a human being!

MY IDENTITY IN CHRIST

> *Therefore, if anyone is in Christ, he is a new creation. The old has passed away; behold, the new has come* (2 Corinthians 5:17 ESV).

MY UNION IN CHRIST

> *. . . Christ in you, the hope of glory* (Colossians 1:27).

LIVING LOVED

Living Loved is not a doctrine to embrace or a discipline to live. No, living loved is not something you accomplish at all. It is a reality you relax into as Jesus takes you by the hand and shows you how … Better Covenant

Discipleship is not about you! It's about God doing His work in and through you. Better Covenant Discipleship is not "How do I build a relationship with God?" but rather "How do I begin to recognize how God is building a relationship with me?" The responsibility is on God. Unfortunately, most of us have believed (wrongly) that the responsibility is on us. Oh my, we are not bright enough to build a relationship with God—man's religion is proof of this![13]

— **Wayne Jacobsen,**
author of *He Loves Me!*
collaborator of *The Shack*

WHO IS CHRIST IN ME?

For many years the question has persisted, ***"Who am I in Christ?"'*** The greater question, however, might be, ***"Who is Christ in me?"'*** Because until you get a revelation of who He is, everything you think about who you are is merely a guess . . .

What we believe, we behold, and what we behold becomes our experience. If you believe you are separated from your Father as a Christian, you will interpret the Bible through the lens of a broken or fragile relationship. However, if you accept that you are "in Him" and that there is no distance, no separation, between you and your Father right now, and that you can't stop the endless flood of His mercy for you, then the Bible stops being a confusing book of conflicting commandments and becomes a beautiful revelation of Love Himself. Being "in Him" doesn't make you God, just as being "in you" doesn't make Him you. However, you are **one**, together. This is a great mystery, but as with many of God's wonders, your heart can know and delight in what your mind may not yet fully understand.

All of Scripture, all of relationships, all of life, all of identity, all of time, every mystery is illuminated in the light of this basic revelation: **You are one with God in Christ by the power of the Spirit.**[14]

> — **Ted Dekker and Bill Vanderbush,**
> authors of *The Forgotten Way Study Guide*

05
WE ARE INCLUDED IN FATHERS'S UNFOLDING PLAN
The Practices of Jesus

UPWARD

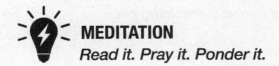

MEDITATION
Read it. Pray it. Ponder it.

> *Every spiritual blessing in the heavenly realm has already been lavished upon us as a love gift from our wonderful heavenly Father, the Father of our Lord Jesus—all because he sees us wrapped into Christ. This is why we celebrate him with all our hearts (Ephesians 1:3 TPT).*

The word **meditate** means to *think deeply or carefully about something, to reflect or ruminate.* Interestingly, rumination is associated with the action of *chewing the cud.* When animals such as cows or sheep *chew their cud*, they **slowly chew their regurgitated, partly digested food over and over again in their mouth before finally swallowing it.** Rumination is a vivid picture of the spiritual practice of Biblical meditation. Meditation, reflection, and memorization implant Scripture deeply into one's heart, soul, and mind. This exercise is vital to getting the truths of God's written word "to stick."

PAUSE AND READ

Ephesians 1:1-14

Grasp the full context of how we're included in our Father's unfolding plan.

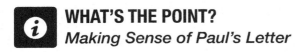 **WHAT'S THE POINT?**
Making Sense of Paul's Letter

Our heavenly Father has an unfolding plan that includes us as His sons and daughters. I love how *The Passion Translation* captures this overarching idea in *Ephesians.* (For this reason, and because of its fresh, readable style, I will reference *The Passion Translation* throughout this study unless otherwise noted.[15]) As you go through this book, take the time to read, ponder and soak in every passage of Scripture. They are not filler; they are the inspired text that gives *Living Loved* its depth of meaning and spiritual authority.

In Ephesians 1:4-6 (TPT), Paul says . . .

> **And he (God) chose us to be his very own,** *joining us to himself even before he laid the foundation of the universe . . .* **It was always in his perfect plan to adopt us as his delightful children, through union with Jesus,** *the Anointed One, so that his tremendous love that cascades over us would glorify his grace—for the same love he has for his Beloved One, Jesus, he has for us.* **And this unfolding plan brings him great pleasure!**

Did you get that? *The same love Father has for Jesus, He has for us.* His unfolding plan is to "include" us—so He's chosen us, adopted us, and wants us to experience intimate union with Jesus, the Christ.

That sounds too good to be true. It's not logical. It's not fair. Exactly! That's why it's called "amazing grace"! This outrageous grace is the foundation of our faith and life in Christ.

Paul continues the introduction of his letter . . .

> *Through the revelation of the Anointed One, he unveiled his secret desires to us—the hidden mystery of* **his long-range plan,** *which he was delighted to implement from the beginning of time* (Ephesians 1:9 TPT).

Please notice that Paul wants to make sure we understand that God has always had a plan that is unfolding. It's a progressive revelation (unveiling) of who God really is and what His intentions are for us (as His children). The good news is that God wants to let us in on His mysterious plan of union and oneness with Himself.

Paul summarizes how God has included us in His unfolding plan in Ephesians 1:11-13 (TPT):

> **Through our union with Christ** we too have been claimed by God as his own inheritance. Before we were even born, he gave us our destiny; **that we would fulfill the plan of God** who always accomplishes every purpose and plan in his heart (v. 11).

Wow! Let that soak in. We are included through our union in Christ. All of the purposes of God's heart are accomplished through Christ living in us and through us!

> God's purpose was that the Jews, who were first to long for the messianic hope, would be the first to believe in the Anointed One and bring great praise and glory to God! And because of him (Christ), when you who are not Jews heard the revelation of truth, **you believed in the wonderful news of salvation . . .** (vv. 12-13).

So, what's the point? God's unfolding plan is to join all humanity to Himself so that we all may experience intimate union with Him through Jesus Christ in the power of the Holy Spirit. The three unified, mutually indwelling persons of God express the blessings of God in the following ways in Ephesians 1.

EPHESIANS 1
Heavenly Father's blessings for His children

- **We have *every spiritual blessing* because we are wrapped into Christ** (v. 3). How incredible is this revelation?

- **He *chose us* to be His very own, joining us to Himself even before He laid the foundation of the universe** (v. 4a). What? Chosen from the beginning?

- **He chose us *to be holy in His eyes with an unstained innocence* because of the Holy One who lives in us** (v. 4b).

- **He *adopted us* as sons and daughters through our union with Jesus Christ, which was always His perfect plan** (v. 5). When this Scripture was written, someone who was *adopted* could never be disinherited. He or she was considered a "forever" son or daughter.

- **He has freely *given us His grace* and love in Jesus** (v. 6).

EPHESIANS 1
Jesus's blessings for all who enter into His life

- **We have *redemption* through His blood shed for our restoration** (v. 7). We've been purchased from the slave market and restored to God's original intent as sons and daughters.

- **We have *forgiveness,* which means the once-for-all, total cancellation of our sins** (v. 7). Did you get that? No more begging, groveling or striving for God's approval. You are forgiven. It's a settled matter, once-for-all.

- **It must be understood that *Jesus Christ is the riches of God's grace.*** Grace is *not something* you and I do or acquire. Grace is Someone. Grace is *Jesus*. Jesus is grace personified. He's all we need. In fact, **Jesus + Nothing = Grace** (vv. 6-8).

- In His life on earth, **Jesus re-presented (incarnated) God in a way that we human beings can understand** (Hebrews 1:1-3). After the cross and resurrection, Jesus now lives *in* and *through* us so we can re-present Him to the world (Colossians 1:27). Truly, Christ is our hope, and we emanate His glory!

EPHESIANS 1
Holy Spirit's blessings for all who are in Christ

- **We have been stamped with the *seal* of the promised Holy Spirit. He now lives inside of us** (v. 13). Romans 8:9 (NIV) says, *"You, however, are not in the realm of the flesh, but are in the realm of the Spirit if indeed the Spirit of God lives in you. And if anyone does not have the Spirit of Christ, they do not belong to Christ."*

- **The Holy Spirit is given to us like an *engagement ring* is given to a bride, as the first installment of what's coming** (v. 14). Ponder this. How does knowing that your are engaged to Jesus change your attitude about yourself?

 **IN**WARD

GRACE REFLECTIONS
Journaling My Thoughts

I am often asked, "When does our salvation occur?" How would you answer this? Let me offer three equally valid answers, from the same one God (in three interpenetrating persons). From the **Father's vantage**, you were saved *when He chose you in Christ in eternity past* (Ephesians 1:4, 11). From **Jesus' vantage**, you were saved *when He died on the cross to redeem and forgive you* (Ephesians 1:7). From the **Holy Spirit's vantage**, you were saved *when you yielded to His conviction (of your unbelief), received Christ as your Savior and your spirit came alive* (Ephesians 1:13; Romans 8:9).

1. What does it mean to you that God the Father has **chosen us** and **adopted us** as sons and daughters through our union with Jesus Christ?

2. Have you ever considered that grace is *not something* you do or acquire? What do you think about the idea that grace is *someone*—Grace is **Jesus**?

3. How might your daily living change if you adopted the idea that the Holy Spirit is given to you like an *engagement ring* is given to a bride, as the first installment of what's coming?

Ponder this: It took three centuries for the Church to come up with a fitting image that would describe the complete nature of God. The Greek word that was chosen is *perichoresis*, which means "to dance around." *Peri* means "around"; and *choresis*, the word that choreography comes from, means "dance." Thus, God was portrayed as the Divine Dance! He is the dance or flow of life that welcomes us to enter into (their) oneness. God is a *circle of shared life* between the Father and the Son in the Holy Spirit.

4. Have you ever thought of God as a community of
    endless, mutual, giving love? Why is this such an
    important reality?

OUTWARD

LIVING LOVED
Experiencing Joy and Overflowing Gladness

We were chosen, adopted, forgiven, and given grace by
God so we can *live loved* and *demonstrate to others
what it means to live loved.* Jesus explained living loved
in this way:

> I love each of you with the same love that the Father loves me.
> **You must continually let my love nourish your hearts**. If you
> keep my commands, you will **live in my love**, just as I have kept
> my Father's commands, for I continually live nourished and
> empowered by his love. **My purpose for telling you these**

things is so that the joy that I experience will fill your hearts with overflowing gladness!

So this is my command: **Love each other deeply, as much as I have loved you.** *For the greatest love of all is a love that sacrifices all. And this great love is demonstrated when a person sacrifices his life for his friends* (John 15:9-13 TPT).

Jesus said that His whole purpose in directing us toward living loved is that we would experience the joy and overflowing gladness that He experiences with His Father. Living loved is not only fulfilling, but it is also Jesus' way of captivating and transforming others.

In John 13:34-35 (TPT) Jesus said . . .

. . . love each other just as much as I have loved you. For when you demonstrate the same love I have for you by loving one another, everyone will know that you are my true followers (disciples).

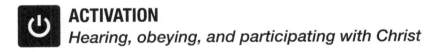

ACTIVATION
Hearing, obeying, and participating with Christ

- What does *living loved* look like for you?

- What adjustments do you need to make in your way of thinking?

- Activation is an *action*. What next step is the Holy Spirit putting on your heart? What's your plan of obedience?

06
PRAYING WITH WISDOM AND REVELATION
Better Covenant Prayer

UP WARD

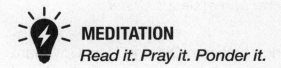

MEDITATION
Read it. Pray it. Ponder it.

> *I keep asking that the God of our Lord Jesus Christ, the glorious Father, may give you the Spirit of wisdom and revelation, so that you may know him better. I pray that the eyes of your heart may be enlightened in order that you may know the hope to which he has called you, the riches of his glorious inheritance in his holy people, and his incomparably great power for us who believe . . . (Ephesians 1:17-19 NIV).*

PAUSE AND READ
Ephesians 1:15-23

Understand how to pray with wisdom and revelation.

WHAT'S THE POINT?
Making Sense of Paul's Letter

Prayer is a vital part of New Covenant living!

It is important to note that Paul prays with a grateful heart, *remembering* the transformation that has occurred in the lives of those in the region of Ephesus. This transformation of faith in the Lord Jesus and love for all God's people has occurred because of one event—*the crucifixion and resurrection of Jesus Christ.*

The primary difference between Old and New Covenant prayer is proximity to the cross event. **Old Covenant prayer** *looks forward* to the Cross/Resurrection and the inauguration of the New and Better Covenant of Jesus. **New Covenant prayer** *remembers* the accomplished work of Jesus and is, therefore, able to offer prayers of thanksgiving that "Jesus' work is finished!"

I have adapted Paul's apostolic prayer in Ephesians 1:15-23, *The Passion Translation,* so we, as New Covenant believers can boldly pray it today. On this side of the cross, our prayers have the authority of the finished work of Jesus Christ. Take a moment to pray through this **Better Covenant prayer**:

> Father, I give thanks for my brothers and sisters in Christ.
>
> I'm grateful for their contagious faith in King Jesus and

tender love for all people that is demonstrated everywhere they go (vv. 15-16).

I thank you Father of glory, that you have revealed yourself to us by Jesus Christ. I ask you to impart your Spirit of **wisdom** and **revelation**, so that we may know You (Father, Jesus, Spirit) more intimately (v. 17).

Father, illuminate the eyes of our imagination, flooding us with your light until we experience the full revelation (unveiling) of the hope of your calling—that is, the **wealth of your glorious inheritances** that you find in us, your holy ones (v.18)!

Father, with our spiritual eyes enlightened, may we continually experience the immeasurable greatness of your power made available to us through faith. May our lives be an advertisement of your immense power as it works through us! Continually remind us that this is the same mighty power that you released when you raised Christ from the dead and exalted Him to the place of highest honor and supreme authority in the heavenly realm (vv.19-20)!

We celebrate the reality that Jesus is now exalted as first above every ruler, authority, government, and realm of power in existence! We rejoice that He is gloriously enthroned over every named that has ever been praised, not only in this age, but in the age that is coming (v. 21)!

Father, you have placed all things under the feet of Jesus, and given Him the highest rank and authority above all others. Jesus Christ alone is the Leader and Source of everything needed in the church (v.22).

And now we declare that we are the church of Jesus Christ! We are the fullness of His body on the earth (v. 23)!

INWARD

GRACE REFLECTIONS
Journaling My Thoughts

As we look back at the finished work of Jesus (grace), our primary requests in Better Covenant prayer today are for our Father to impart His wisdom and revelation to us. **Wisdom** is deep understanding from the Spirit. **Revelation** is the unveiling of the mysteries of grace (Jesus). The Spirit reveals the **goodness of God** and **our inclusion** and **inheritance in Christ.**

1.   What's the difference between Old and New Covenant prayers? Why is this significant?

2.   Who are some of the people you are thankful for because of their contagious faith in Jesus and tender love for people (vv. 15-16)? Take a moment to offer thanks for them.

3. Your life is an advertisement of God's immense power as it works through you. The question is, what kind of an advertisement is your life (vv. 19-20)?

4. Are you aware of the authority and power you have inherited because of your union in Christ (vv. 20-22)?

OUTWARD

LIVING LOVED
New Covenant Prayer

One of the most freeing things I have ever discovered is the power of New Covenant prayer. For many years, I longed to pray *with* God, not merely pray *toward* God. I longed for deep conversation with my heavenly Father, but because I had no real understanding of the finished work of Jesus, I struggled to understand what a gift prayer truly is. Because I lived with a mixture of Old and New Covenant understanding, my prayer life was weak and uncertain. Shame, guilt, and fear were my constant companions. Prayer quickly became a drudgery instead of a delight. Instead of enjoying fellowship with my Father through Jesus in the anointing of the Holy Spirit, most of my time and energy was spent wondering if I was doing enough to please my God. Truthfully, in my mind, God was more a disapproving judge than a loving Father.

Fear was causing me to throw my prayers up to God and then quickly get out of the way.

What I longed for was a prayer experience where I felt relaxed and at home with my heavenly Dad. I desired to have a relationship in which I felt safe enough to spend hours in His presence, experiencing and reciprocating His love. I wanted to know Father-Jesus-Holy Spirit personally and intimately—no longer a slave to fear, but as an adopted son and co-heir with Christ (Romans 8:15-17).

I wanted to experience God's amazing grace in my prayer life. Oh, I had experienced the grace of salvation, but now I needed grace to live out my salvation and its promised freedom. I desperately needed the empowering Presence of God in my life. I felt like the folks of Galatia that Paul addressed. *I had begun by means of the Spirit and was now trying to finish by means of the flesh (Galatians 3:3).*

When I discovered that God's grace is to be applied to every area of life, the shift that began to take place in my thinking was dramatic! I began to reevaluate my whole life. The most important question was no longer, "Lord, what should I do?" but rather, "Lord, what do I truly believe about You, myself, and others?" and "What are You doing and how do you want me to join You?"

In time, I would discover the vital importance of understanding the true heart of God and the New Covenant He is currently engaged in with mankind because of the accomplished work of Jesus. Truly believing and trusting in the once-for-all forgiveness of my sin that Jesus provides, and His resurrection life and power now inside of me, have been the game-changer in my communion and communication with God.

I now pray from a place of *being loved* and *living loved.* Prayer is now about abiding in Jesus, cultivating sensitivity to the Spirit, and asking my loving heavenly Father to impart His wisdom and revelation regarding whatever I'm going through.

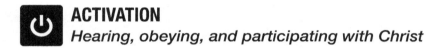

ACTIVATION
Hearing, obeying, and participating with Christ

- **What is God saying to you?**

- How does your prayer life need to change?

- What adjustments do you need to make in your way of thinking?

07
SAVED BY GRACE
My New Identity in Christ

UPWARD

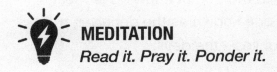
MEDITATION
Read it. Pray it. Ponder it.

> *For it is by grace you have been saved,*
> *through faith—and this is not from*
> *yourselves, it is the gift of God—not by*
> *works, so that no one can boast*
> *(Ephesians 2:8-9 NIV).*

PAUSE AND READ
Ephesians 2:1-10

Understand what it means to be saved by grace.

WHAT'S THE POINT?
Making Sense of Paul's Letter

In Genesis 2, we learn that there were two trees in the
middle of the garden of Eden: the *tree of life* and the *tree*
of the knowledge of good and evil. These two trees,

planted in the midst of God's created paradise, represent two choices set before humanity. The **tree of life** represents God's intended best—the choice of Father-Son-Spirit as one's source of life. The **tree of the knowledge of good and evil** represents God's loving prohibition (Genesis 2:17)—the choice of human intellect and reasoning as one's source. Agreement with tree of life means agreement with God, His purposes and His ways. Agreement with the tree of knowledge means agreement with the one known as the deceiver, the accuser, the father of lies—the devil.

For those who choose the tree of knowledge, the issue is always "right or wrong" or "good or bad." The tree of life, however, is always concerned with the greater issue of "life or death." So, when Jesus came into our darkness, He offered us His light and life.

He came to restore the true image of God and the purpose of mankind as His sons and daughters.

Paul picks up the themes of life and death and God's restoration plan of grace in Ephesians 2. He starts by comparing our old nature, before our "in Christ" encounter, with our new nature in Christ. Our old nature is the result of tree-of-knowledge living; our new nature is the result of tree-of-life living, which was made possible through the forgiveness and redemption of Jesus.

OLD NATURE

Paul declares that we were once like corpses, dead in our sins. **Sin** is a break in God's intended relationship with us. Sin is always our choice or agreement with someone's word, other than God's. It's a killer! Eating from the wrong tree and agreeing with the wrong voice will always end in death—the absence of life (Ephesians 2:1).

There are two major off-roads of the world: *rebellion* and *religion*. **Rebellion** is man's declaration of independence from God, while **religion** is one's best attempt to appease and please God with his or her performance and good works. Neither work. Paul says that we followed the world's religion, customs, and values and came up empty (Ephesians 2:2).

Man's pattern has been to obey the dark ruler of the earthly realm, and satan works overtime in the hearts of those who are disobedient to the truth of God. He is the master of illusion (Ephesians 2:2).

When we become controlled by the desires of **self-life,** then the cravings of our flesh and the **distorted thinking** of our mind take over. It's obvious to all that our old nature is deserving of God's wrath. Our only hope is realignment with God (Ephesians 2:3).

BUT GOD

But God still loved us with such great love. He is so rich in compassion and mercy. Even when we were dead and doomed in our many sins, he united us into the very life of Christ and saved us by his wonderful grace (Ephesians 2:4-5 TPT).

Two of my favorite words in Scripture are "**but God . . .**" We've all been there. We are at our absolute worst . . . we are at wit's end . . . we are deserving of punishment . . . **but God** still loved us and is rich in compassion and mercy. That's always the backdrop of God's wonderful grace.

NEW NATURE

Because of God's great love and grace, we are now united into the very life of Christ; we are restored to our original identity. We are alive! Plain and simple, we have been saved by His wonderful grace (Ephesians 2:5).

At the cross event, we were co-crucified with Christ (Galatians 2:20). After the cross, we were co-resurrected with Christ, the exalted One, and we ascended with Him into the glorious perfection and authority of the heavenly realm, where we are now co-seated as one with Christ. Our new identity in Christ will be the visible display (throughout the ages) of the infinite, limitless riches of God's grace (Ephesians 2:6-7).

This is Paul's summary of this section:

> For it was only through this **wonderful grace** that we believed in him. Nothing we did could ever earn this salvation, for it was the **gracious gift from God** that brought us to Christ! So no one will ever be able to boast, for salvation is never a reward for good works or human striving. We have become his poetry, a re-created people that will fulfill the destiny he has given each of us, for we are joined to Jesus, the Anointed One. Even before we were born, God planned in advance our destiny and the good works we would do to fulfill it (Ephesians 2:8-10 TPT—emphasis mine).

INWARD

 GRACE REFLECTIONS
Journaling My Thoughts

Remember that **rebellion** is your declaration of independence from God and **religion** is your best attempts to appease or please God with your performance and good works.

1. Which path are you most prone to take as a substitute for a relationship with God? Explain.

2. In Hebrews 6:1 (KJV), we are told to repent from **dead works.** A dead work is *anything that is not initiated or energized by God.* In other words, we must repent from living from the fruit of the tree of knowledge. (Consider this: a **good work** *that is not initiated or empowered by the Spirit is a* **dead work** —the wrong tree!) What is the Spirit bringing to mind of which you need to repent?

3. How has satan proven to be a master of illusion in your life?

4. What does it mean to be united into the very life of Christ?

5. What is keeping you from reaching your full potential? (See Ephesians 2:6-7 TPT.)

6. **Digging Deeper.** What do the following phrases mean to you?

    • "Co-crucified with Christ"—

    • "Co-resurrected with Christ"—

    • "Co-seated as one with Christ"—

OUTWARD

♥ LIVING LOVED
Being Always Precedes Doing

Love is the fulfillment of all the law. Religion, however, turns Father's love into a performance-based effort.

For the majority of my life I believed that it was my own righteousness that earned the love of the Father. After years of striving to attain Father's love, I finally woke up to the realization that the love of the Father transforms me and makes me holy from the inside out. My holiness is an "inside job." It is the work of the Holy Spirit who lives inside of me, not of any work I can do myself. My performance could never make me holy or righteous; only the abiding relationship with the Holy One who lives in me and emanates from me makes me holy.

This is why in the Kingdom of God "being must always precede doing."

Grace is an invitation to a relationship with God, not a doctrine or a license to live any way you choose to live. Real freedom is the empowering presence of God in your life that enables you to be whom you were created to be, and to do what you have been called to do.

Once grace is established as the core of our being, we are then empowered to join God in what He is doing (Ephesians 2:8-10).

ACTIVATION
Hearing, obeying, and participating with Christ

- **What is God saying to you?**

- **What does *living loved* look like to you right now?**

- What adjustments do you need to make in your way of thinking?

08
ALL WELCOME
A New Humanity

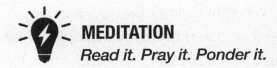

MEDITATION
Read it. Pray it. Ponder it.

> *For he himself is our peace, who has made the two groups one and has destroyed the barrier, the dividing wall of hostility, by setting aside in his flesh the law with its commands and regulations. His purpose was to create in himself one new humanity out of the two, thus making peace, and in one body to reconcile both of them to God through the cross, by which he put to death their hostility . . .*
> *(Ephesians 2:14-16 NIV).*

PAUSE AND READ
Ephesians 2:11-22

Understand what it means to live in unity and oneness with Christ and others.

For a deeper understanding of Ephesians 2:15, consider Paul's powerful words in Colossians 2:13-15.

ℹ WHAT'S THE POINT?
Making Sense of Paul's Letter

Paul now specifically addresses the work of Christ for those who were not born as Jews. Though most of the believers in the Ephesian church were Gentiles (non-Jews), they knew that much of God's program in the Old Testament involved the Jews.

In Genesis 12, God (Yahweh) called Abraham and his heritage (Jews) to be a *unique* and *blessed* people. They were to be an example and a blessing to the Gentiles by helping them understand Yahweh's purposes and ways. Unfortunately, this is not how it turned out. Instead of being a *blessing*, the circumcised Jews looked down their noses at the uncircumcised Gentiles. For centuries the Jews displayed an attitude of arrogance and superiority toward others that God had never intended.

Ephesians 2:12 NIV describes what it feels like to be an "outsider" (Gentile). The Gentiles felt they were:

- **Separate from Christ.** The Ephesians worshiped the goddess Artemis, and before the coming of the Gospel message, knew nothing about Jesus Christ.

- **Excluded from citizenship in Israel.** The Jews were a very exclusive community. It was virtually impossible to break in to their circle.

- **Foreigners to the covenants.** God did not make covenants with Gentile nations. They were "aliens" and "strangers." They were *without hope* and *without God.*

BUT NOW
The Good News for All of Us

> *But now* in Christ Jesus you who once were far away have been brought near by the blood of Christ (Ephesians 2:13 NIV— emphasis mine).

"But now in Christ Jesus . . ." This is God's miraculous intervention for *all* mankind!

We all need it; none of us can earn it. We were all *far away.* **But now . . . suddenly** everything has changed. Everything is new! *God has come near!* God is now with us as Jesus (Immanuel). Jesus Christ has brought us near by His blood and *included us all* in His New Covenant. Did you get that? We are included. We belong to the family of God, and it's all because of the welcoming grace of Jesus.

A NEW HUMANITY
Ephesians 2:14-18 (TPT)

Reconcile means "to bring together again." Jesus' peace mission is to reconcile Jews and non-Jews to God and to each other. *The Passion Translation* conveys it this way:

> *Our reconciling "Peace" is Jesus! He has made Jew and non-Jew one in Christ. By dying as our sacrifice, he has broken down every wall of prejudice that separated us and has now **made us equal through our union with Christ . . . forming one new humanity, Jews and non-Jews fused together*** (Ephesians 2:14-15 TPT— emphasis mine.)

Paul continues,

> *For the Messiah has come to preach this sweet message of peace to you . . . and **now because we all are united to Christ, we both have equal and direct access in the realm of the Holy Spirit to come before the Father*** (Ephesians 2:17-18 TPT— emphasis mine.)

Let that sink in! Because we are united to Christ, we have direct access to the Father in the realm of the Holy Spirit! Are you picking up on how important *reconciliation*, *peace, union,* and *unity* (oneness) are in the economy of the Kingdom of God? Unity is incredibly powerful because UNITY IS THE HEART OF GOD!

> *How good and pleasant it is when God's people live together in unity . . . For there the Lord bestows his blessing, even life forevermore* (Psalm 133:1-3 NIV).

THE FAMILY OF GOD
Ephesians 2:19 (TPT—emphasis mine)

> *So, you are not foreigners or guests, but rather you are the children of the city of the holy ones, with **all the rights as family members** of the household of God.*

Paul is saying that because of Jesus' finished work on the cross, the door to the family has been flung wide open. There's now a sign that reads: ALL WELCOME! That's right; even the most marginalized, dehumanized outcasts; even you and me— we are welcome to the Family.

Jesus is our elder brother and the one who has made a way for us. Interestingly, the early church called themselves the Way. This was not an arrogant or prideful designation; rather, it was a humble admission that without Jesus I'm sunk. I'm not going to make it without Jesus' inclusive rescue. Jesus is not only my way of hope, He is the Way of hope to all. In Him ALL are welcome!

THE TEMPLE OF GOD
Ephesians 2:20-22 (TPT—emphasis mine)

> ***You are rising like perfectly fitted stones of the temple;** and your lives are being built together upon the ideal foundation laid by the apostles and prophets, and best of all, you are*

*connected to the Head Cornerstone of the building, the
Anointed One, Jesus Christ himself!*

*This entire building is under construction and is continually
growing, under his supervision, until it rises up completed as
the holy temple of the Lord himself. This means that **God is
transforming each one of you into the Holy of Holies, his
dwelling place, through the power of the Holy Spirit living
in you!***

Because the temple curtain was torn at the last breath of
Jesus, you and I are now the Temple. Better yet, we are
the Holy of Holies; we now host the very Presence of
God (1 Corinthians 6:19-20).

INWARD

GRACE REFLECTIONS
Journaling My Thoughts

Recall a time when you felt like an "outsider" (not
included, didn't belong). Separation is so painful
because its origins are the devil.

1. What do you do when you feel separated from
   Christ? When you feel without hope?

Stop for a moment to read and meditate on Romans 8:35-39 (TPT—emphasis mine). Let it seep into your soul:

Who could ever separate us from the endless love of God's Anointed? Absolutely no one! For nothing in the universe has the power to diminish his love toward us. Troubles, pressures, and problems are unable to come between us and heaven's love. What about persecutions, deprivations, dangers, and death threats? No, for they are all impotent to hinder omnipotent love, even though it is written, All day long we face death threats for your sake, God. We are considered to be nothing more than sheep to be slaughtered!

Yet even in the midst of all these things, we triumph over them all, for God has made us to be more than conquerors, and his demonstrated love is our glorious victory over everything!

So now I live with the confidence that there is nothing in the universe with the power to separate us from God's love. I'm convinced that his love will triumph over death, life's troubles, fallen angels, or dark rulers in the heavens. There is nothing in our present or future circumstances that can weaken his love. **There is no**

power above us or beneath us—no power that could ever be found in the universe that can distance us from God's passionate love, which is lavished upon us through our Lord Jesus, the Anointed One!

2. Is separation from God ever a reality *(on this side of the cross)*? What is the Spirit is saying to you in Romans 8:35-39?

3. Do you think of yourself as the new Holy of Holies, a place that hosts the Presence of God? Explain.

Adopting the new mindset *(thinking of yourself as the new Holy of Holies, a place that hosts the Presence of God)* will help you shift from a separation mentality to one of inclusion.

4. Do you tend to be **inclusive** or **exclusive** in your view of others? Do you believe Jesus came to rescue all people *(i.e. Muslims, Hindus, Buddhists, Atheists, etc.)*? Explain.

5. Does your view of Jesus put Him in a box? Is your Jesus big enough? Explain.

6. Unity means I'm a part of something bigger than myself. Imagine yourself as a "living stone" being fit together with other specially fashioned stones to be a holy temple for the Lord Himself. Does this view of unity inspire you to live with greater purpose and meaning?

OUTWARD

LIVING FREE
The Upside-Down Kingdom

Jesus' path to freedom and victory is always different than the world's path. The apostle John referred to Jesus as "the lamb of God who takes away the sin of the world." He accomplished His mission by demonstrating the way of the Lamb. In other words, Jesus embodied "reconciling peace" in a world that exerts violence.

Israel's religious leaders of the day longed for a Messiah who would overcome its Roman oppressors through military might and power. But Jesus introduced the way of a new, upside-down Kingdom (of God) based on reconciliation, forgiveness, peace, and unity.

Brian Zahnd states:

> The cross is a cataclysmic collision of violence and forgiveness. The violence part of the cross is entirely human. The forgiveness part of the cross is entirely divine. God's nature is revealed in love, not violence. The Rome cross was an instrument of imperial violence that Jesus transformed into a symbol of divine love.[16]

The Lamb of God defeated the Beast of Rome through the power of forgiveness, grace, and peace. The same Lamb that reconciled the world to Himself (2 Corinthians 5:19) also made Jew and non-Jew one in Christ.

> ***Our reconciling "Peace" is Jesus! He has made Jew and non-Jew one in Christ.*** *By dying as our sacrifice, he has broken down every wall of prejudice that separated us and has now made us equal through our union with Christ . . .* ***forming one new humanity,*** *Jews and non-Jews fused together* (Ephesians 2:14-15 TPT).

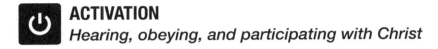

ACTIVATION
Hearing, obeying, and participating with Christ

- Whom do you need to include, forgive, or extend God's peace to?

Two books that have challenged me to personally "get in the game" regarding reconciliation, forgiveness and peace are *Be the Bridge (Pursuing God's Heart for Racial Reconciliation)* by Latasha Morrison and *People to be Loved (Why Homosexuality is not Just an Issue)* by Preston Sprinkle. Both of these books go beyond information to activation. Remember, activation is *an action*.

- What next step is the Holy Spirit putting on your heart? How will you participate with Christ in what He is doing around you?

09
GOD'S MYSTERIOUS PLAN OF GRACE
Our Secret Weapon

UPWARD

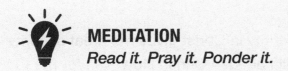

MEDITATION
Read it. Pray it. Ponder it.

> *This mystery is that through the gospel the Gentiles are heirs together with Israel, members together of one body, and sharers together in the promise in Christ Jesus (Ephesians 3:6).*

PAUSE AND READ
Ephesians 3:1-12

Understand God's mysterious plan of grace.

WHAT'S THE POINT?
Making Sense of Paul's Letter

In Chapter 3 of Ephesians, Paul continues his discussion of God's unfolding plan to include all of mankind in His life and purposes. He uses the word mystery or secret to describe the nature of God's plan. **Mystery**, as used by Paul, means *something that is formerly hidden (veiled) but is now revealed (unveiled).*

Many of us say we like a good "mystery," but the truth is, mystery can be very frustrating. Why? Because *a mystery from God cannot be understood except by* ***divine revelation*** (Ephesians 3:3). Mystery is just an indicator that I need a fresh revelation from Father.

The truth is, my identity in Christ gives me great security —I am and have all I need in Christ. However, for me to "grow up" spiritually, I must continually receive new revelation of who God truly is and who I am because of my union in Christ.

This revelation comes from my intimate union with Christ (John 15:5). Therefore, I must learn to trust God with mystery, for it's an invitation to intimacy—an opportunity to get to know Father-Jesus-Spirit better!

OUR PRIVILEGES
Ephesians 3:5-6 (TPT—emphasis mine)

As New Covenant and Kingdom of God people, we have privileges that no prior generation has ever had.

There has never been a generation that has been given the detailed understanding of this glorious and divine mystery until now. He kept it a secret until this generation. God is revealing it only now to his sacred apostles and prophets by the Holy Spirit. **Here's the secret: The gospel of grace has made you, non-Jewish believers, into co-heirs of his promise through your union with him. And you have now become members of his body—one with the Anointed One!**

Did you see the mystery in v. 6? The mystery that was hidden (veiled) but has now been revealed is this: the Gospel of grace is available to all! The Gospel of grace has included non-Jewish believers as co-heirs of Jesus' promises through their union with Him. Both Jews and non-Jews are a part of the body of Christ and inheritors of all of His promises. Think about it—salvation is available for all!

PAUL'S PASSION
Ephesians 3:7-9 (TPT—emphasis mine)

I have been made a messenger of this wonderful news by the gift of grace that works through me. Even though I am the least significant of all his holy believers, this grace-gift was imparted when the manifestation of his power came upon me. Grace alone empowers me so that I can boldly preach this wonderful message to non-Jewish people, sharing with them the unfading, inexhaustible riches of Christ, which are beyond comprehension. **My passion is to enlighten every person to this divine mystery. It was hidden for ages past until now and kept a secret in the heart of God, the Creator of all.**

Paul's passion and purpose were to host the Presence of God (Father-Jesus-Spirit) in such a way that they would captivate the curiosity, hearts, and minds of everyone with whom he came in contact. We, too, are called to "enlighten every person to the divine mystery that *all are included* because Jesus died that *all* may live loved, live free, and live full."

GOD'S PURPOSE
Ephesians 3:10-12 (TPT—emphasis mine)

> The **purpose of this was to unveil** before every throne and rank of angelic orders in the heavenly realm God's full and diverse wisdom revealed through the church. This perfectly **wise plan was destined from eternal ages and fulfilled completely in our Lord Jesus Christ**, so that now we have boldness through him, and free access as kings before the Father because of our complete confidence in Christ's faithfulness.

Paul's summary is that the perfect unfolding plan of God (from eternal ages) has been fulfilled completely in Jesus Christ. Now all are welcome and included! We are a part of God's royal priesthood. We are royalty.

Did you notice—"*Now we have boldness through him, and **free access as kings** before the Father because of our complete confidence in Christ's faithfulness*" (v. 12)? We are kings because of Jesus' faithfulness. And, hallelujah, our Father is the King of kings (that's us)!

INWARD

GRACE REFLECTIONS
Journaling My Thoughts

1. When you hear the word "mystery," what comes to mind?

2. What has God most recently revealed to you about Himself?

3. For what things in your life are you currently seeking revelation?

4. Do you have a passion to "enlighten every person to the divine mystery that *all are included* because Jesus died that *all* may live loved, live free, and live full"?

5. Do you see yourself as royalty with free access to come before your Kingly Father?

OUTWARD

LIVING FREE
God's Secret Battle Plan

"Mystery" is a word used by the apostle Paul throughout his various letters. Unfortunately, the true meaning of the Greek word *musterion* was lost for centuries after Paul's initial writings. In the last 100 years, *musterion's* original meaning has been recovered through archaeological findings associated with a Macedonian Greek royal family, which ruled the Ptolemaic Kingdom in Egypt from 305-30 BC.

Findings revealed that *musterion* (mystery) was a term referring to "a secret battle plan," known only to the king. At the last moment the king would disclose the battle plan *to* and *through* his sons, who were the acting generals of his army. The Ptolemies became famous for their use of this secret battle strategy to defeat their enemies.

Paul likely borrowed the concept behind *musterion* to describe God's secret battle plan that was ordained before the beginning of the ages but was revealed (unveiled) at the coming of the King's Son—Jesus.

In fact, Paul makes this bold statement: "This mystery (God's secret battle plan and eternal blueprint) was kept hidden for ages, but has now been made known to me so that I can reveal it to you" (Ephesians 3:3-5). In essence, Paul is saying that only those who are now sons (and daughters) of the New Covenant in Christ the Son have received this revelation.

Why did God hide the mystery? Mike Bickle has said, "There is a divine strategy in the way God unfolds hidden information, that binds our hearts to Him and enlarges us in even greater love." In other words, mystery is an invitation to intimacy!

Paul unveils four secret weapons (mysteries) that give us victory over satan, his lies, accusations, deceptions, and their resulting shame, guilt, fear, and condemnation. Take time to meditate on each of these **four Secret "in Christ" Weapons**:

- **Weapon #1 My New Covenant in Christ accomplished at the cross** (1 Corinthians 2:6-10). The cross event unveiled the mystery of God's *forgiveness* and *redemption* for mankind.

- **Weapon #2 My New Union in Christ** (Colossians 1:25-27). On this side of the cross, the Spirit of Christ lives inside of all believers (Romans 8:9), offering new *hope*, *identity,* and *purpose*.

- **Weapon #3 One New Humanity in Christ** (Ephesians 3:3-6; Romans 16:25-27; Colossians 2:2-3; Colossians 4:3-4). Unlike the **Old Covenant**, in the **New Covenant** *all* are welcome and fellow heirs in Christ! *All* are included *and* accepted. The Gospel is for all!

- **Weapon #4 Our New Identity as the Bride of Christ** (Ephesians 5:32; Revelation 19:7-9). We have infinite value and worth as eternal companions with Jesus!

These secrets are available to us today to enforce the victory that is already ours. The key questions are "to whom are we listening and with whom are we agreeing?" We must remember that we are not fighting *for* victory; we are fighting *from* victory (in Christ). The Good News is that the victory has been won!

Jesus is our secret battle plan (Galatians 4:4-9 NIV). His coming into our darkness and inviting us into His light and life (John 1) changed everything! The spiritual life is an ongoing revelation of what it means to live in union with Christ. There is nothing "deeper" than life in Christ!

 ACTIVATION
Hearing, obeying, and participating with Christ

- How does seeing *mystery* as God's secret battle plan reshape your perspective, thinking, and identity? How will this change the way you will live?

- ## How will you utilize your **four Secret "in Christ" Weapons?**

  ### Weapon #1
  My New Covenant in Christ accomplished at the cross. (See I Corinthians 2:6-10.)

  ### Weapon #2
  My New Union in Christ. (See Colossians 1:25-27.)

Weapon #3

One New Humanity in Christ. (See Ephesians 3:3-6.)

Weapon #4

Our New Identity as the Bride of Christ. (See Ephesians 5:32; Revelation 19:7-9.)

10
PRAYER TO BE ROOTED IN LOVE AND POWER
Better Covenant Prayer

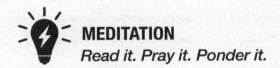

MEDITATION
Read it. Pray it. Ponder it.

> *I pray that out of his glorious riches he may strengthen you with power through his Spirit in your inner being, so that Christ may dwell in your hearts through faith. And I pray that you, being rooted and established in love . . . (Ephesians 3:16-17 NIV).*

PAUSE AND READ

Ephesians 3:14-21

Understand how to pray in love and power.

WHAT'S THE POINT?
Making Sense of Paul's Letter

Ephesians 3:16-21 is Paul's second prayer in this letter. I have adapted it into a prayer we can pray today.

EPHESIANS 3:14-15 (OUR POSTURE)

Paul describes his heart attitude and posture in prayer:

> **So I kneel humbly in awe before the Father of our Lord Jesus, the Messiah,** *the perfect Father of every Father and child in heaven and on earth* (Ephesians 3:14-15 TPT).

This must have been quite an experience for the Roman soldier chained to Paul. While there is no prescribed posture for prayer, Paul chooses to kneel in an expression of sheer awe and honor of his Father and Savior.

Take a moment to pray through this New Covenant prayer, from both an individual and corporate vantage. While potent as a personal prayer, this apostolic prayer was written to a group of believers. There is tremendous power in unity and unified prayer.

Ephesians 3:16-21 (Adapted from TPT):

Father, I pray that You would unveil within me (us) the

unlimited riches of Your glory and favor until supernatural strength floods my (our) innermost being with divine might and explosive power (v. 16).

I pray that the **life of Christ will be released deep inside of me (us) through the constant use of my (our) faith.** I pray that the resting place of Your love will become the very source and root of my (our) life (v. 17).

Father, I thank you for empowering me (us) to discover what every holy one experiences—the great magnitude of the **astonishing love of Christ in all its dimensions**. Jesus, I am grateful for Your deeply intimate and **far-reaching love!** I'm grateful for how **enduring and inclusive Your love is!** It's an **endless love** beyond measurement that transcends my (our) understanding. **Your extravagant love** pours into me (us) until I am filled to overflowing with the fullness of God (vv. 18-19).

Father, I (we) will never doubt **Your mighty power to work in me (us) and through me (us) to accomplish Your purposes.** I (we) believe You will achieve infinitely more than my (our) greatest request, my (our) most unbelievable dream, and exceed my (our) wildest imagination! Father, **Your miraculous power constantly energizes me (us)** (v. 20).

Father, I (we) offer up to You all the glorious praise that rises
from every church in every generation through Jesus Christ,
for ever and ever! Amen (v. 21).

INWARD

GRACE REFLECTIONS
Journaling My Thoughts

1. What did God reveal to you as you were praying
   this prayer as an individual?

2. What did God show you as you prayed from a
   corporate perspective *(us and we)*?

3. Did you notice that the life of Christ is released as we exercise our faith muscle? What does this mean to you?

4. How many of these dimensions of the love of Christ have you experienced? Give an example.

   Deeply intimate love of Christ?

   Far-reaching love of Christ?

   Enduring love of Christ?

   Inclusive love of Christ?

   Endless love of Christ?

   Extravagant love of Christ?

5. What are some ways you have experienced the mind-blowing power of God?

OUTWARD

LIVING LOVED
*Seeing Through a **Covenant Lens***

One of the primary reasons I struggled in prayer is because I saw prayer as more of a transaction than a relationship. I saw prayer as more of a duty than a delight. In short, I was trapped in an Old Covenant mindset. My view of God was through a legal lens. I saw God primarily as a *judge*. Furthermore, I saw myself as a *guilty defendant*. I saw Jesus as *my defense lawyer*. The endgame to me was *acquittal*, which meant eternal life in heaven one day when I die. This view was reinforced by the fact that I have always lived in a Western "contract" culture.

A contract is about *legal rights* and is based on mistrust and liability. If I don't get what's legally mine—I'll sue you!

God's way is much different. He relates to us through a *covenant lens.* A covenant lens sees God primarily as a *good Father.* He sees humanity as a *wayward, lost bride.* Jesus is our *Bridegroom* in search of His lost bride. The endgame is *oneness with Jesus (*and Father in the anointing of the Spirit), which means eternal life begins with a relationship of "knowing" God (John 17:3).

A contract is quite different than a covenant. It is motivated by either fear or incentive, while a covenant is motivated by love (1 John 4:19).

Covenant love changes everything! If we view our relationship through a contract lens, everything we believe will be contrary to God's way of grace.

For instance, a **contractual** teaching of the Gospel says, "You must repent to be forgiven!" The focus is on what *we* must do, our action. A **covenantal** understanding of the Gospel says, "Because I am forgiven (by the once-for-all crucifixion of Jesus), therefore, I repent (change my way of thinking to align with God's way of thinking)."

The *contract lens* sounds completely logical. And it would be if forgiveness (salvation) were up to us! But, the truth is, repentance is a byproduct (fruit) of God's forgiveness.

The Gospel is better than we ever dreamed. Once the eyes of our hearts are enlightened to the reality of the *accomplished work of our salvation*, we will begin to believe this reality in our *hearts*. Naturally, this bubbles up out of our souls and through our *mouths* with the confession "Jesus is Lord—He's now my Lord!" (Romans 10:9-10).

What if many in the West have gotten the Gospel wrong?

What if the Good News is *really* good news? What if the Gospel is *really all* about Jesus (grace personified)?

Could it be that we in the West are so enamored with *contracts* that many have missed the whole point of God's New Covenant in Jesus?

I believe it's time we return to Better Covenant living— completely—beginning with the really good news of the New Covenant.

New Covenant prayer is primarily giving thanks for all that was accomplished in Jesus' finished work of grace and asking for greater revelation of all that entails.

Truly, the way we "see" God determines the way we communicate with God!

Do you need a lens adjustment?

ACTIVATION
Hearing, obeying, and participating with Christ

- Are your prayers based on covenant love or contractual obligation? How do you need to adjust your way of praying?

- Ask Father for an upgrade in your experience of His love and power.

- Who is God putting on your heart?

HALFTIME

WORSHIP BREAK

I've played sports all my life. When playing football in high school, I considered halftime as a welcomed and cherished respite from the game.

Halftime is a time to rest, reset, and refocus before returning to the game! I think this equates well with the purpose of worship gatherings. In 1 Peter 2:9, disciples of Jesus are called a royal priesthood. The role of a kingly priest is two-fold:

1. To **minister to** the heart of God. This is why the component of worship is so vitally important. Our role, plain and simple, is to bless the heart of God! *Worship is not an emotional response to a style of music that makes me happy.* No, true worship (in whatever form) ministers to the heart of God.

2. To **minister from** the heart of God. The worship gathering of royal priests is a sabbath break from the ordinary to *minister to* the Extraordinary One so we can then be launched back into the "game of life" to *minister from* the heart of God. As royal

ambassadors, we carry the Kingdom with us wherever we go. Ministering from the heart of God is "participating" with God where He is at work.

This segment of the book, *Halftime*, is a time to **review** the first half of *Ephesians* and **prepare** for the second half. While the first half is more theological and foundational, the second half is very practical—grace in action!

REVIEW

The first three chapters of *Ephesians* deal primarily with spiritual realities and truth surrounding our **identity** and **union** in Christ.

First Half

Chapter 1
Our Identity in Christ

Chapter 2
Our Unity in Christ

Chapter 3
The Mystery of Grace

HALFTIME

Are you ready for the second half? It will be a little more "in your face"! For instance, the next chapter is entitled "Let's Grow Up!"

My spiritual mentor likes to say, "Discussing theology is great, but '*doing* it is doing it.' Reading about it is *not* doing it . . . even praying about it is *not* doing it. '*Doing* it is doing it!'"[17] Participating with God requires obedience (faith and action)—that's *doing* it! Are you ready for the second half?

PREVIEW

The next three chapters of Ephesians explain how we are to live a pure and powerful life through our **union** and **authority** in Christ.

	Chapter 4:1-16 **Our Unity in Christ**
	Chapter 4:17-5:17 **Our Purity in Christ**
Second Half	Chapter 5:15-6:4 **Our Harmony in Christ**
	Chapter 6:10-20 **Our Authority in Christ**

⏻ ACTIVATION
Hearing, obeying, and participating with Christ

Take ten to fifteen minutes—right now—for a worship break to *minister to the heart of God.*

- Why must *ministering to* the heart of God always precede *ministering from* the heart of God? How are you doing?

- What does daily worship (ministering to the heart of God) look like for you?

- How will you minister from the heart of God this week? Be specific. And remember, "*doing it* is doing it!"

Part III
LIVING FREE

Living Free describes *Christ's life in me* (Colossians 1:27). As a New Covenant disciple of Jesus, I emanate His life everywhere I go! My purity flows from my identity and union in Christ, while grace serves as the source of my identity and union in Christ.

It's vital to understand that my purity (holiness) flows from the *Holy* Spirit who lives within me (1 Corinthians 6:19-20). As an ambassador of Christ, I am free from a life of striving because I now live free in Christ!

MY PURITY IN CHRIST

Do you not know that your bodies are temples of the Holy Spirit, who is in you, whom you have received from God? You are not your own; you were bought at a price. Therefore honor God with your bodies (1 Corinthians 6:19-20 NIV).

MY GRACE IN CHRIST

For it was only through this wonderful grace that we believed in him. Nothing we did could ever earn this salvation, for it was the gracious gift of God that brought us to Christ! So no one will ever be able to boast, for salvation is never a reward for good works or human striving (Ephesians 2:8-9).

DISCOVERING WHO YOU ALREADY ARE

God now no longer deals with sin, having accomplished that end in the finished work of Christ. Now He is solely occupied with our righteousness. Every situation provides us with the opportunity to remain in our chosen standing in Christ. We abide in Him. We learn to walk in newness of life. We stay dead! We have permission to consider ourselves dead to sin but alive to God.

We do not become new persons by changing our behavior. We discover the person we already are in Christ and behave accordingly. Eyes of honor are fixed not only on *what Jesus has done for us*, but also on *who He is right now* in this chapter of our lives. Everything is about training in righteousness, goodness, loving-kindness, grace, mercy, and honor. Every circumstance is concerned with the stance for Christ we are going to take in our lives.

Identity is the echo of belief. It is our identity in Christ that is always being challenged. We are new creations. All the old has passed away and all things have become new.[18]

— **Graham Cooke,**
author and speaker

11
LET'S GROW UP
Maturity, Unity, Diversity

MEDITATION
Read it. Pray it. Ponder it.

For the Lord God is one, and so are we, for we share in one faith, one baptism, and one Father. And He is the perfect Father who leads us all, works through us all, and lives in us all (Ephesians 4:5-6 NIV).

PAUSE AND READ
Ephesians 4:1-16

Understand God's intention for the Church to exhibit maturity, unity and diversity.

ⓘ WHAT'S THE POINT?
Making Sense of Paul's Letter

Paul gets to the practical application of his letter in Ephesians 4. He seems to be saying, "In light of the fact that you've been blessed with every spiritual blessing (Ephesians 1), God's amazing grace (Ephesians 2), and His supernatural revelation (Ephesians 3)—it's now time for you to grow up!"

Ephesians 4:14-16 (NIV) is the heart of the chapter:

> . . .**Then we will no longer be infants**, *tossed back and forth by the waves, and blown here and there by every wind of teaching and by the cunning and craftiness of people in their deceitful scheming.* **Instead, speaking the truth in love, we will grow to become in every respect the mature body of him who is the head, that is, Christ.** *From him the whole body, joined and held together by every supporting ligament, grows and builds itself up in love, as each part does its work.*

It's all right to be a baby, if you indeed are a baby. But when you have to part the whiskers to put the baby bottle in one's mouth, it's time to grow up!

The world is full of people who are out to catch you when you are emotionally fragile and recruit you to their particular brand of teaching. Therefore, we must grow up so we can recognize any deception that is not grounded in Jesus.

MATURITY
Ephesians 4:13-16 (NIV)

We must all grow up and reach our full potential—that's what it means to reach maturity. In Ephesians 4:13, we learn that maturity consists of three things:

- **Unity in the faith.** This is oneness without prejudice. This oneness causes us to work together, each doing his own part (v.16).

- **The knowledge of Jesus.** This is a deep knowing and intimacy with Jesus.

- **The whole measure of the fullness of Christ.** This carries the idea of bearing the full image of Christ and re-presenting Christ to the world as His ambassador.

Don't stay stuck or stunted. Don't be self-centered, independent, or childish—GROW UP!

If you are "practicing the presence of Christ" moment by moment, you will not make "soft" choices in difficult circumstances or blindly follow people with wrong thinking.

UNITY
Ephesians 4:1-6 (NIV)

Unity is the state of being united or joined as a whole. It carries the idea of oneness and harmony. Notice, the word "one" is used eight times in Ephesians 4:2-6.

> *2 Be completely humble and gentle; be patient, bearing with* **one** *another in love.* *3 Make every effort to keep the unity of the Spirit through the bond of peace.* *4 There is* **one** *body and* **one** *Spirit, just as you were called to* **one** *hope when you were called;* *5* **one** *Lord,* **one** *faith,* **one** *baptism;* *6* **one** *God and Father of all, who is over all and through all and in all* (NIV— emphasis mine).

In this section, Paul is referring back to what he wrote in Ephesians 2:14-22 and 3:6. He's presenting the picture of a "blended" family. Two cultures are becoming one, leaving generations upon generations of prejudice (prejudgment) behind to become one new humanity with a new common Father and Elder Brother.

Today there is absolutely no separation. There is no division in Christ! There is . . .

ONE BODY.

ONE SPIRIT.

ONE HOPE.

ONE LORD.

ONE FAITH.

ONE NEW IDENTITY *identified with Christ in baptism.*

ONE FATHER.

ONE NEW HUMANITY *in Christ.*

DIVERSITY
Ephesians 4:7-12

The Kingdom of God has boundless variety and diversity. And it's all important and valuable. Jesus' death and resurrection were for ALL humanity. This inclusiveness means many very different types of people, each having many different gifts.

In Ephesians 4:7 (NIV), Paul writes, "But to each one of us grace has been given as Christ apportioned it." He uses the Greek word *hekasto* (which means "each, every") to describe Jesus' distribution of grace. In essence, Paul is saying "each and every one of us gets to play in the Kingdom of God." Every individual receives custom-made grace from God! Therefore, everyone's unique contribution matters!

God loves diversity and "uniqueness." For this reason, Paul writes . . .

> *We do not dare to classify or compare ourselves with others . . .*
> (2 Corinthians 10:12 NIV).

There is absolutely no need to compare ourselves to others because we get our own unique assignment and the necessary gifting to fulfill it from God! If we focus on our assignment, we won't have time to be jealous of what others are doing.

In his book *The Ruthless Elimination of Hurry,* John Mark Comer writes, "Comparison eats away at our joy, doesn't it? Whatever your thing is— there will always be somebody better at it than you. Always. Stings, doesn't it? But why should it? . . . when did the standard for success become a celebrity's magnum opus, not our own sweat and tears?"[19] If we stay in our own lane, or better yet the lane God has given us, we will be fruitful and fulfilled.

Paul lists five specific gifts that Christ gave for the purpose of equipping (preparing) His people for works of ministry so that the body of Christ may be built up, strengthened, and enlarged (Ephesians 4:12). We will examine these in detail in the next chapter.

Like every good parent today, Jesus intended for all of His children to grow up and find their fit in His family!

INWARD

GRACE REFLECTIONS
Journaling My Thoughts

1. Think back to your childhood. Did a peer or someone who was just a few years older than you ever say, "You are so immature. You need to grow up"? How'd it make you feel?

2. Have you ever had someone you highly respect challenge you to grow up? Describe that encounter.

3. Ponder how the Lord is challenging you in the following areas.

- **Unity:** What prejudices must you relinquish to include others?

- **Intimacy:** Are you making room for God? Are you in too big a hurry? Are you "practicing the presence of God" moment by moment?

- **Diversity:** Whom do you need to reach out to who is different than you?

- **Ministry:** Are you ministering *from* the heart of God or from obligation?

4. Do you struggle with comparing yourself and your accomplishments with others? Why is this unwise and unhealthy?

5. Why do you think *oneness* is so important to God?

 **OUT**WARD

LIVING FREE
The Power of Oneness

Oneness is not only the theme of Ephesians 4:1-16, it's God's master plan for all mankind. From the beginning, God desired a people that would live in intimate union with Himself.

In fact, Jesus' entire rescue mission is about oneness. In the final chapters of John's gospel, Jesus makes this crystal clear:

> *My prayer is . . . that all of them may be one, Father, just as you are in me and I am in you. May they also be in us so the world may believe you have sent me. I have given them glory that you gave me, that they may be one as we are one—I in them and you in me—so that they may be brought to complete unity. Then the world will know that you sent me and have loved them even as you have loved me* (John 17:20-23 NIV).

Let that sink in! Jesus' prayer for believers is that we would enter into oneness with Him and Father in the power of the Spirit. And from that union, believers would grow in unity with others. Through unified love, the whole world will ultimately know what God and His love look like—*oneness, union, unity!*

This theme of oneness is why I chose the **triquetra symbol (trinity knot)** on the front cover of this book. It pictures the mutual, unbreakable union between Father, Son and Spirit. And it also portrays the union and unity God desires us to have with Him and others.

As I was meditating about union and oneness while on sabbatical a few years ago, I felt the Spirit prompt me to get a tattoo. Though I had considered it for years (fifty-six years to be exact), I knew it would have to be something of extraordinary importance for me to mark my body with it. The triquetra, which I now bear on my inner forearm, is a daily reminder of my extraordinary union with God and others.

Unity is the primary theme of *Ephesians.* Because unity is so transformative, the devil works overtime to erode it and cause separation and division.

On a personal level, satan makes us feel like we are separated from God. This is perhaps the greatest LIE of all because it robs us of our security and identity in Christ. (See Romans 8:31-39.)

On a corporate level, it's reported that there are more than 40,000 Christian denominations today. The wonderful diversity (Ephesians 4:7-16), which was meant to display the multifaceted beauty of the body of Christ, has been exploited by satan, causing the Church to be divided, disconnected, and separated by both comparison and the counterfeit of unity—uniformity.

I praise God that the Church is waking up to the devil's schemes and rediscovering her true identity and unity in Christ.

In my city and region, we are seeing a growing movement of unity as congregations gather in concerted union to cover the I-35 corridor with unceasing prayer. Pastors of different streams are putting aside differences and uniting together, as *Pastors in Covenant* and *Be the Bridge* small groups are beginning to spring up. Competition and comparison are giving way to honest conversation and mutual care. One group member said it well: "PIC groups are safe places where joys are doubled, burdens are halved, and life flows freely."

Jesus said the world would come to know Him through the way we display His love in our unity!

⏻ ACTIVATION
Hearing, obeying, and participating with Christ

- Is God putting anyone on your heart with whom to reach out *(hangout)*? What might this look like?

- Is He putting anyone on your heart with whom to start a prayer group? What might this look like?

- Is He putting anyone on your heart with whom to start a study of this book? What might that look like?

12
FIVE-FOLD EXPRESSION OF CHRIST

Discovering How I Express Jesus

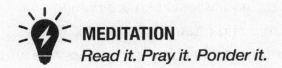 **UP**WARD

MEDITATION
Read it. Pray it. Ponder it.

> *So Christ himself gave the apostles, the prophets, the evangelists, the pastors and teachers, to equip his people for works of service, so that the body of Christ may be built up until we all reach unity in the faith and in the knowledge of the Son of God and become mature, attaining to the whole measure of the fullness of Christ (Ephesians 4:11-13 NIV).*

PAUSE AND READ

Ephesians 4:11-13

Understand the five-fold expressions of Christ.

ⓘ WHAT'S THE POINT?
Making Sense of Paul's Letter

Paul specifically focuses on five different **gifts of Christ** that will equip and edify (strengthen) His Church until we all attain *unity in faith,* until we all experience *intimacy with Christ,* and until we all become one, displaying the full dimensions of spiritual *maturity in Christ* (Ephesians 4:11-13).

Neil Cole, Alan Hirsch, and Mike Breen are pioneers in the field of discipleship and organic church life. These men have been instrumental in shaping my language and descriptions of the five grace gifts of Christ: apostles, prophets, evangelists, shepherds, and teachers (APEST). Each of these gifts represents a different expression that Christ exemplified during His ministry on earth.

Re-presenting Jesus as He truly is to our onlooking world is our purpose as disciples of Christ. Therefore, we will dive a little deeper to discover the role of each gift and help activate you in your place in the body of Christ.

Apostles. An apostle is one who is sent out to be *a culture changer* and *dream awakener.* Apostles function as the *eyes* of the church—they help the church "see through an apostolic lens." Mature apostles function as spiritual fathers and mothers— mending what is broken, supplying what is lacking, and ordering what is disordered.

They lead in a way that not only builds, strengthens, and equips the body of Christ, but also empowers and activates others to lead from their gifting.

An apostle will ask these types of questions: "Are we helping people step into their destiny?" "Is our city and region being transformed?" "Are we pioneering new works?" "Are we raising up sons and daughters who are Kingdom people?"

Prophets. Prophets are *heart revealers*. They function as the ears of the church—helping her to "hear and obey the voice of God." They inspire and encourage a contagious prophetic culture in the entire body of Christ.

Prophets work in tandem with apostles, laying a firm foundation for the church (Ephesians 2:20). Their deep spiritual insight builds, strengthens, and equips the body of Christ.

Prophets ask these types of questions: "Are people hearing God's voice and obeying?" "Are we cultivating a prophetic culture?" "Are people being activated in their prophetic gifting?"

Both apostles and prophets are focused on bringing heaven to earth!

Evangelists. Evangelists are *Good News tellers.* They are the *mouth* of the church because they delight in sharing the Gospel with those who are not-yet believers. As with each of the five expressions of Christ (APEST), there are many different types of evangelists. Alan Hirsch and Tim Catchim describe four different types of evangelists: *investors, inviters, convincers, and conversers.*

> *Investors* walk with people through the entire process of conversion, from friendship to conversion and beyond in an ongoing discipling relationship. *Inviters* woo others to accompany them into strategic environments that allow greater exposure to Jesus. *Convincers* make convincing and persuasive presentations of the gospel. *Conversers* gradually expose people to the message in ways that allow them to process and internalize its meaning for their lives.[20]

Evangelists are treasure hunters, for they see and call out the best in all people, even those who appear beyond hope. Evangelists carry the heart cry of Jesus— that all be saved.

Evangelists ask, "Are new people entering the Kingdom of God?" "How can we demonstrate Christ's love to all people?"

Shepherds. Shepherds are *soul healers.* They represent the *arms* of the church, extending care and compassion to believers. Shepherd is translated *pastor* (i.e., pasturer) in many translations, but for clarity I am using the word *shepherd*. Interestingly, the word "pastors" is used only one time in the New Testament . . . only one time, and it's in Ephesians 4:11-12. In current Western church culture, pastors abound:

We have Lead Pastors, Associate Pastors, Worship Pastors, Executive Pastors, College Pastors, Family Pastors, Youth Pastors . . . I think you get the point!

Pastor is a function, not a title for a ministry staff position. In fact, few church leaders are primarily gifted as pastors (pasturers). So today's language of "Pastor of Parking" really confuses what Paul is actually saying. (Thanks for allowing me to rant a bit.)

A mature shepherd asks, "Are the people of God caring for and loving one another?" "Are people finding their 'fit' in the body of Christ?"

Both evangelists and shepherds are focused on people. Evangelists are primarily concerned with connecting not-yet believers to Jesus and His family. Shepherds are primarily concerned with the health and growth of believers.

Teachers. Most of us are well acquainted with teachers. We've had them since we can remember. In Paul's mind, teachers are *light givers.* They appeal to the *mind*— explaining, enlightening, and activating the body of Christ. Revelatory teachers are treasure hunters in the sense that they "unveil" the truth of New Covenant living.

Teachers ask, "Are people feeding on the written and living Word of God?" "Are people rooted in their understanding of the New Covenant and the Kingdom of God?"

Teachers are a "bridge" between apostles/prophets (God's heart) and evangelists/pastors (man's heart). They unveil God's written word (Scripture) and the Living Word (Jesus) so mankind can experience the Kingdom of God on earth as it is in heaven!

GRACE REFLECTIONS
Journaling My Thoughts

I remind you of Paul's words in Ephesians 4:7, *"But to each one of us* [Greek: *hekasto] grace* has been given as Christ apportioned it." *Hekasto* literally means "to each and every person"—everyone gets to play (not just the professionals)!

> **NOTE:** These gifts of Christ come in "seed form." So, one must grow to maturity in each of these equipping gifts before he or she will be asked to equip others. So, when I say *everyone gets to play*, please understand that I'm speaking of "playing within your personal season of maturity." For example, in baseball, few get to the major leagues, but at the beginner level, virtually everyone gets to play and many are called upon to be a coach or manager.

1. **With which of the five expressions of Christ do you most resonate? Why?**

    Apostle - *Culture changer*   **Prophet -** *Heart revealer*
    Evangelist - *Good News teller*   **Shepherd** - *Soul healer*
    Teacher - *Light bringer*

2. Who are some mature equippers/practitioners who come to mind in each of the five gifts of Christ?

> **Apostle** - *Culture changer*

> **Prophet** - *Heart revealer*

> **Evangelist** - *Good News teller*

> **Shepherd** - *Soul healer*

> **Teacher** - *Light bringer*

3. How do you most naturally share your faith?

Investor?   *Inviter?*   *Convincer?*   *Converser?*

OUTWARD

LIVING FREE
Discovering How I Express Jesus

One of the most helpful tools I've found to help others discover their gift(s) of Christ is Mike Breen's eighty-question, online, five-fold survey. Go to the link below and take a few minutes to answer this survey. Your score will be calculated for you immediately. I believe it could be very helpful in discovering and confirming how you best express Jesus.

ACTIVATION
Hearing, obeying, and participating with Christ

- What is God saying to you?

FiveFoldSurvey.com by Mike Breen and 3DM

- What are you learning about yourself? How will you "step into your position" on the team?

- Who is someone of like passion and wiring that you can learn from?

13

THE TRUTH, THE LIFE, THE WAY

Putting Off the Old and Putting On the New

UPWARD

MEDITATION
Read it. Pray it. Ponder it.

> *You were taught, with regard to your former way of life, to put off your old self, which is being corrupted by its deceitful desires; to be made new in the attitude of your minds; and to put on the new self, created to be like God in true righteousness and holiness (Ephesians 4:22-24 NIV).*

PAUSE AND READ

Ephesians 4:17-32

Understand the power of putting off the old and putting on the new in order to become a mature disciple of Christ.

ⓘ WHAT'S THE POINT?
Making Sense of Paul's Letter

In John 14:6 Jesus said, *"I am **the way** and **the truth** and **the life**. No one comes to the Father except through me."* In Ephesians 4:17-32, Paul unpacks instructions for Kingdom-living the Jesus way.

The Truth. Paul begins this section of his letter by addressing the absolute importance of right *thinking!* The truth is, Jesus has acquired our freedom at the cross, yet the devil has used an array of lies to keep us from receiving the full freedom that is ours. The primary lie of satan is about our new identity in Christ. If we do not understand the truth of what Jesus accomplished for us, we will fail . . . repeatedly.

In short, most men and women don't know who they are, and this is why they don't live rightly.

> *. . . **You should not live like the unbelievers around you who walk in their empty delusions.** Their corrupted logic has been clouded because their hearts are so far from God—their blinded understanding and deep-seated moral darkness keeps them from the knowledge of God* (Ephesians 4:17-18 TPT—emphasis mine).

The NIV says, *". . . you must no longer live as Gentiles (unbelievers) do, in the futility of their thinking. They (unbelievers) are darkened in their understanding and*

*separated from the life of God because of their ignorance
. . . due to the hardening of their hearts."*

The point is, Spirit-indwelled believers have a new
identity. We are new creations in Christ (2 Corinthians
5:17). Paul expounds in his letter to the *Romans:*

> *Therefore do not let sin reign in your mortal body so that you*
> *obey its lust . . . For sin shall not master over you, for you are*
> *not under law, but under grace* (Romans 6:12,14 NASB).

Jonathan Welton writes, "We are powerful . . . We are not
victims or slaves of sin as we once were. If we sin, it is
because we choose to . . . When we choose to believe
what God says about us, we are enabled to receive His
grace for righteous living (Romans 5:17). When we
accept His truth about us, we no longer strive for
approval through works. Rather, we simply accept God's
declaration of our righteousness. As God renews our
minds according to this truth, we will begin to access the
grace to live righteously."[21]

Paul finishes his thoughts on the importance of living
from the truth of who we are in Christ by explaining the
progression of unbelief (v. 19): Loss of sensitivity to God
(spiritual apathy) soon becomes giving oneself over to
sensuality and the indulgence in every kind of impurity,
greed, and sexual obsession.

The Life. Paul continues, *"But this is not the **way of life** that Christ has unfolded within you. If you have really experienced the Anointed One, and heard his **truth**, it will be seen in your life; for we know that the ultimate reality is embodied in Jesus!"* (Ephesians 4:20-21TPT— emphasis mine).

The indwelling life of Christ is the Source of our new life (Colossians 1:27). So what is this way of life that Jesus has unfolded to us and within us? How do we walk the way of Jesus?

The Way. In Ephesians 4:22-32, Paul gives us the answer to how we are to walk the way of Jesus in two phrases—***put off your old self*** and ***put on the new self.*** Here's what that looks like:

Put off the old self . . . let go of the lifestyle of the ancient man, the old self-life, which was corrupted by sinful and deceitful desires that spring from delusions (v.22).

Put on the new self . . . be made new by every revelation that's been given to you . . . be transformed as you embrace the glorious Christ within as your new life . . . live in union with Him. Embrace the reality that you have been re-created by God in His perfect righteousness and holiness (vv.23-24).

In Ephesians 4:25-32, Paul gets specific about how to live in the way of Christ:

Put off dishonesty and lying. Be known as one who speaks the truth and promotes unity (v. 25).

Put off anger and the desire for revenge. Be quick to resolve conflict. Do not give the devil a foothold (vv. 26-27).

Put off stealing. Be industrious, earning an honest living, and then you'll have enough to bless those in need (v. 28).

Put off ugly and hateful words. Let your words become beautiful gifts that encourage others (v.29).

Do not grieve or take for granted the Holy Spirit. Always honor the Holy Spirit of God who has sealed you until you experience your full salvation (v. 30).

Put off bitter words, temper tantrums, revenge, profanity, and insults. Be kind and affectionate to one another, forgiving each other (v. 32).

INWARD

GRACE REFLECTIONS
Journaling My Thoughts

1. Why do you think satan's primary tactic is to distort our way of thinking and confuse our minds?

I find it interesting that Jesus' first message was, *"The time has come; the kingdom of God has come near. **Repent** and believe the good news"* (Mark 1:15 NIV).

Repent (Greek: *metanoia*) means to *"change your way of thinking."* In essence, Jesus was declaring that His coming signaled a moment in time when everything changed. He is Lord, and worthy of our full trust and allegiance. But in order to believe in Him, we must first change the way we think. We must *put off* our old way of thinking.

2. What do you need to **put off** (let go of)?

    - Describe how you struggle with dishonesty and lying.

    - Describe how you wrestle with anger and desire for revenge.

- **Describe ways that you wrestle with stealing or dishonesty.** *Do you take what doesn't belong to you or do you fail to return things that you borrow?*

- **Describe ways you struggle with using hateful language** *(i.e. profanity, foolish talk, coarse joking or slander)* **that hurts others.**

- What are some ways that you struggle with unforgiveness, bitterness and being easily offended?

- What are some ways that you are critical or judgmental?

- In conflict are you Passive? Aggressive? Passive-Aggressive? Assertive? Explain.

Assertive people can separate the person from the problem. They care more about the person than being right or having the person like them.

When we choose to believe what God says about us, we are enabled to receive His grace for righteous living.

We are transformed as we **"put on" the indwelling Christ as our new life.** In time, the reality settles in that we have been re-created by God in His perfect righteousness and holiness. Then the Truth, the Way, and the Life can be lived out.

OUTWARD

 LIVING FREE
The Importance of Water Baptism

The importance of baptism can be pictured by considering the three most important events in human existence—birth, marriage, and funeral, or as my friends in England say when one is *hatched*, *matched*, and *dispatched*.

Baptism is a birth announcement. It declares new life!

Who does most of the work in childbirth? The one being born simply agrees to be pushed out from darkness into the light.

> But when the kindness and love of God our Savior appeared, He saved us, not because of righteous things we had done, but because of His mercy. He saved us through the washing of rebirth and renewal by the Holy Spirit (Titus 3:4-5 NIV).

Baptism is a wedding covenant. It is connected with the power of covenant (oneness)!

Baptism in the New Covenant has the same purpose as circumcision in the Old Testament. It's a covenant seal/

sign. Jesus circumcises (cuts off) our "old self" through baptism (Colossians 2:10-15).

Water baptism is an external, visible sign of making a break with the past. Much like a wedding ring, water baptism says, "I'm off the market; I belong to Jesus now."

Baptism is a funeral. It declares that my old self is dead and needs to be buried!

Paul makes this point in Romans 6:1-11 (NIV—emphasis mine):

*What shall we say, then? Shall we go on sinning so that grace may increase? By no means! We are those who have **died to sin**; how can we live in it any longer? Or don't you know that all of us who were baptized into Christ Jesus were **baptized into his death**?*

*We were therefore buried with him through **baptism into death** in order that, just as Christ was raised from the dead through the glory of the Father, we too may live a new life. For if we have been **united with him in a death like his**, we will certainly also be **united with him in a resurrection like his**. For we know that our **old self was crucified** with him so that the body ruled by sin might be done away with, that we should no longer be slaves to sin—because anyone who has died has been set free from sin. If we **died with Christ**, we believe that we will also live with him. For we know that since Christ was raised from the dead, he cannot die again; death no* *longer has mastery over him. The death he died, he died to sin once for all; but the life he lives, he lives to God. In the same way, **count yourselves dead to sin but alive to God in Christ Jesus.***

Did you get it?

We have been co-crucified with Christ, and **our old man is dead, dead, dead.**

We have been co-resurrected with Christ, and **our new identity screams out, "Alive in Christ!"**

Paul wants to make sure we "get it," so he uses the word *dead* (to our old self) fourteen times in Romans 6:1-13. That's emphatic! My old self is dead, and I'm alive in Christ!

Water baptism is the "picture" of what it looks like to *put off your old self* and *put on the new self*.

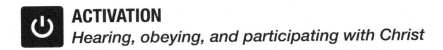

ACTIVATION
Hearing, obeying, and participating with Christ

- What is God saying to you?

- Have you been water baptized? If yes—take a moment to remember your baptism. If you have never been baptized (with the full understanding of its meaning and purpose), have a conversation with someone (pastor, mentor, fellow disciple) about being baptized (Acts 22:16).

14
PURITY IN CHRIST with Joel Lowry
Holiness and Communion

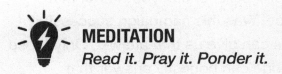

MEDITATION
Read it. Pray it. Ponder it.

> *. . . walk in the way of love, just as Christ loved us and gave himself up for us as a fragrant offering and sacrifice to God. But among you there must not be even a hint of sexual immorality, or of any kind of impurity, or of greed, because these are improper for God's holy people (Ephesians 5:2-3 NIV).*

PAUSE AND READ

Ephesians 5:1-4

Understand that our purity (holiness) comes from the Holy Spirit who lives in us.

ⓘ WHAT'S THE POINT?
Making Sense of Paul's Letter

In April 1993, an international Christian group formed *True Love Waits* (TLW) to promote sexual abstinence outside of marriage for teenagers and college students. The first year of the campaign, over 102,000 young people signed a pledge. At the end of the decade, approximately 2.5 million American youth took the pledge of abstinence. Was this campaign successful? I don't think numbers can give us that answer. Only those who signed the pledge can honestly answer that question.

One thing I do know is that a relationship with *the rules of holiness*, instead of a relationship with *the spirit of holiness*, leads to either rebellion or religion—and both are a miserable way to live.

In Ephesians 5:2-3 (NIV), Paul writes . . .

> **. . . walk in the way of love, just as Christ loved us and gave himself up for us as a fragrant offering and sacrifice to God.** *But among you there must not be even a hint of sexual immorality, or of any kind of impurity, or of greed, because these are improper for God's holy people.*

The way of love is a life lived like Christ. But how is this possible?

It's actually impossible for most of us to do the preceding verses—"follow God's example, as dearly loved children and walk in the way of love" (Ephesians 5:1-2 NIV). Why? Because most of us read "follow" through an Old Covenant lens. We think we need to "work harder, to be better." But the truly Good News is that as born-again believers, Christ now lives in us and minds His Kingdom business through us!

The good news is my purity is not in my external actions, but rather in my new identity in Christ.

My holiness (innocence, purity) comes from the Holy Spirit who lives inside of me (1 Corinthians 6:19-20).

Joel Lowry has said, "Purity is not about a list; it's about stewarding my end of a relationship. It's about *resting in the way of love* (v. 2). However, when we are wounded in our sexuality, it prohibits our ability to love others in a healthy manner. For instance, sex drive is a good thing, but it must be stewarded well in order to have a healthy intimate relationship."[22]

In Genesis 2, God created man as the object of His love and affection. Genesis 2:21 is most accurately translated "God separated Adam in half." He separated masculinity and femininity and then brought them back together. He bound them together by covenant love. By definition, a covenant is a binding agreement, through the act of cutting, for the purpose of "oneness."

Lowry continues, "Sex outside of marriage creates a covenant connection without the *protection* of covenant vows and commitment. This is why Paul says *sexual immorality* and *lust* (impurity) are improper for God's holy people (Ephesians 5:3). In our brains we actually *bond* with the person with whom we have sexual intercourse. This opens us up to an illegitimate connection that does not have the protection that covenant provides."

You might want to read the preceding paragraph again. Read it slowly. Let the truth soak in. It might just rescue you from a world of unnecessary hurt and pain.

It's interesting that in Jewish culture, purity was (and is) sacred. The act of *sealing wedding vows* was not giving a "kiss" or "ring"; rather, the sealing of the vows was done through the sacred act of sexual intercourse.

In 1 Corinthians 6:15-20 (NIV), Paul addresses the issue of sexual immorality head-on:

> ***Do you not know that your bodies are members of Christ himself? Shall I then take the members of Christ and unite them with a prostitute? Never!*** *Do you not know that he who unites himself with a prostitute is one with her in body? For it is said, "The two will become one flesh." But whoever is united with the Lord is one with him in spirit. Flee from sexual*

immorality. All other sins a person commits are outside the body, but whoever sins sexually, sins against their own body. Do you not know that your bodies are temples of the Holy Spirit, who is in you, whom you have received from God? You are not your own; you were bought at a price. Therefore honor God with your bodies.

God's prohibition of sex before marriage is a protection. He wants each of us to experience intimacy without shame. He wants us to be so free of shame that we can give ourselves completely in covenant to our spouse, as He intended.

INWARD

GRACE REFLECTIONS
Journaling My Thoughts

1. "A relationship with *the rules of holiness,* instead of a relationship with *the spirit of holiness,* leads to either rebellion or religion." Does this statement reflect your personal experience? Explain.

2. Why is sex outside of marriage so dangerous? (Reflect on your own experience.)

3. Ponder (discuss with someone): "Why is shame so powerful? Long-lasting?"

4. "Sex is *not* about you and what you *receive*. No, it's about what you *give* to the other person." How would your marriage (or future marriage) be different if you and your spouse took this to heart?

5. In light of 1 Corinthians 6:15-20, why is it so important to understand sexuality within the context of God, oneness, and spirituality?

6. What is something new that you learned? A question you're pondering?

OUTWARD

LIVING FREE
Holiness & Communion (Joel Lowry)

HOLINESS

The Holy Spirit is the Spirit of holiness. "Holy" is not merely a description of the Spirit; it is also a description of the work the Holy Spirit does in us. *We are holy because the Holy Spirit lives inside us.* He is our identity!

Let me say it as clearly as I can: *If you've been violated and abused, know this—nobody can take your innocence.* Only you can choose to give it away.

God wants to set ALL of us free from shame! The glory of the Gospel is that God can restore us. Relationship with *rules* of holiness, instead of the *spirit* of holiness, will make you miserable. But the Holy Spirit empowers the impossible.

Sex is *not* about you and what you **receive** (let that sink in). No, it's about what you **give** to the other person. Sex is a gift that brings connection. Within the marriage covenant, it's incredible. Outside of marriage covenant protection, it can be incredibly destructive.

COMMUNION

Ponder This. Sex is to human relationship (covenant oneness) what Holy Communion is to our relationship with God (New Covenant oneness).

- Communion is an act of "renewing my commitment to God" and "re-upping my vows with Him."

- Communion is a celebration of my/our "common-union" with God (Father, Son, Spirit).

- Communion is celebrating my/our "restoration to innocence" by the blood of His cross. Listen to this:

And by the blood of his cross, everything in heaven and earth is brought back to himself— back to its original intent, restored to innocence again (Colossians 1:20 TPT).

A major concept in Paul's writings is **justification.** Justification means "to be declared innocent." We have obtained a "salvation of innocence," which is much different than being declared "not guilty." Not guilty leaves us open to the snare of *shame.*

Justification (declared innocent) restores my heart and mind to clean and pure because of the Holy One inside me.

. . . all are justified freely by his grace through the redemption that came by Christ (Romans 3:24).

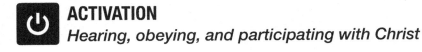

ACTIVATION
Hearing, obeying, and participating with Christ

- **What is God saying to you?**

- What adjustments do you need to make in your way of thinking?

- Are you being robbed of your destiny because of shame? Rethink, renounce the lie, and receive the fullness of God's *restoration and justification,* which restores your innocence and makes you clean and pure. Ask the Holy Spirit for a fresh baptism of innocence!

15
LIVING LIKE JESUS
The Practices of Jesus

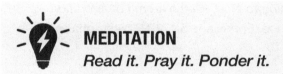

MEDITATION
Read it. Pray it. Ponder it.

> *Be imitators of God in everything you do, for then you will represent your Father as his beloved sons and daughters. And continue to walk surrendered to the extravagant love of Christ, for he surrendered his life as a sacrifice for us. His great love for us was pleasing to God, like an aroma of adoration —a sweet healing fragrance (Ephesians 5:1-2 TPT).*

PAUSE AND READ
Ephesians 5:1-18

Understand how to live like Jesus.

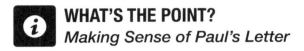

WHAT'S THE POINT?
Making Sense of Paul's Letter

THE WAY OF LOVE

> *Be imitators of God in everything you do, for then you will* **represent your Father as his beloved sons and daughters.** *And continue to walk surrendered to the extravagant love of Christ, for he surrendered his life as a sacrifice for us. His great love for us was pleasing to God, like an aroma of adoration—a sweet healing fragrance* (Ephesians 5:1-2 TPT—emphasis mine).

Re-presenting our Father accurately is our calling (v.1). At first this looks like imitating the ways of God. Jesus even said, ". . . the Son can do nothing by Himself; He can do only what He sees His Father doing, because whatever the Father does the Son also does" (John 5:19 NIV). Children imitate their parents until they are mature enough to make wise decisions themselves. As children of God, we come to maturity when we are born again, receive the Holy Spirit, and begin hosting the One who lives within us.

In essence, as we grow in our life with the Spirit, our imitating of our Father becomes the emanating of His indwelling Spirit! This is what it means to walk in the way of love.

THE WAY OF LIGHT

> *Once your life was full of sin's darkness,* **but now you have the**
> **very light of our Lord shining through you because of your**
> **union with him.** *Your mission is to live as children flooded with*
> *his revelation-light! And the supernatural fruits of his light will be*
> *seen in you—goodness, righteousness, and truth* (Ephesians
> 5:8-9 TPT—emphasis mine).

Our mission is to leave the gravitational pull of darkness
and live fully immersed in the revelation-light of our union
with Jesus. The result of living from oneness with Jesus
is that we begin to emanate His identity of goodness,
righteousness, and truth.

> *And don't even associate with the servants of darkness*
> *because they have no fruit in them; instead, reveal truth to*
> *them. The very things they do in secret are too vile and filthy to*
> *even mention. Whatever the revelation-light exposes, it will also*
> *correct, and everything that reveals truth is light to the soul*
> (Ephesians 5:11-13 TPT).

As light-filled sons and daughters, our primary purpose
is to be so full of life and truth that it awakens others
who are in a deadly slumber. We are to expose
lifelessness, correct lies, and become "light to every soul
we encounter."

THE WAY OF WISDOM

*So be very careful how you live, not being like those with no understanding, but **live honorably with true wisdom,** for we are living in evil times. Take full advantage of every day as you spend your life for his purposes. And don't live foolishly for then you will have discernment to fully understand God's will* (Ephesians 5:15-17 TPT-emphasis mine).

We all want to know what the wonderful will of God is for our lives. Paul says the secret to understanding God's will requires true wisdom: living life with purpose and supernatural understanding. This is very different than the world's wisdom. The world says, "You only go around once, so eat, drink and be merry!"

The wisdom of God says,

*And don't get drunk with wine, which is rebellion; instead **be filled with the fullness of the Holy Spirit*** (Ephesians 5:18 TPT--emphasis mine).

The key to Better Covenant living is the fullness of the Spirit found in Ephesians 5:18. The wine of the world is only a substitute for the wine of the Spirit. The joy of being inebriated in the Spirit's fullness always surpasses the momentary joy of drinking too much wine. And the fruit of each? It's your choice: love, joy, peace, patience. . . or a huge hangover!

INWARD

GRACE REFLECTIONS
Journaling My Thoughts

WAY OF LOVE

The starting place to spiritual maturity is *knowing experientially* how much you are loved by God (Father-Son-Spirit). We love others in the same way we receive God's love for us.

1. One example of living loved is the practice of gratitude. Who are three people for whom you are grateful? Why?

WAY OF LIGHT

2. How do you escape the gravitational pull of darkness (shame, fear, guilt, scarcity, comparison, etc.)?

3. Walking in the light (being vulnerable, open, and transparent) exposes darkness. Dr. Brené Brown states, "Vulnerability (uncertainty, risk, and emotional exposure) is the birthplace of love, belonging, joy, empathy, innovation, creativity, faith and courage! It disempowers shame, scarcity, and comparison."[23] Where do you need to embrace vulnerability?

WAY OF WISDOM

4. How might you live your life with greater purpose
    and intentionality?

LIVING FREE
The Practices of Jesus

Jesus was rarely in a hurry. Yes, His schedule was full,
yet He never appeared to be hurried—giving off "busy
signals." Jesus understood the *unforced rhythms of
grace* that allowed Him to be truly present in each
moment.

In *The Ruthless Elimination of Hurry,* John Mark Comer
writes, "Jesus made sure to inject a healthy dose of
margin in his life. 'Margin is the space between our load
and our limits' . . . He would get up early and go off to a

quiet place to be with his Father . . . Every chance he got, he would enjoy a nice long meal with friends over a bottle of wine, creating space for in-depth conversations . . . He would practice Sabbath on a weekly basis—an entire day set aside for nothing but rest and worship, every single week . . . and notice his practice of simplicity . . . he lived freely and lightly."24

Jesus lived with healthy rhythms, and so should we. Jesus had practices that served as pathways of grace. They were means to an end, not the end themselves. Much like an athlete practices and disciplines himself in order to win, we too must practice spiritual disciplines to access the grace that indwells us as disciples.

"A discipline is a way to access power . . . A spiritual discipline is creating time and space to access God himself at the deepest level of your being."25 I would add, then His Spirit within you will emanate the *life* of Christ to others.

In this same book, Comer mentions four practices of Jesus that are helpful for us today:

- **Silence and solitude.** The art of coming back to God and our true self.

- **Sabbath.** A restful, grateful life of ease, appreciation, wonder, and worship.

- **Simplicity**. Freedom and focus on what matters most.

- **Slowing**. The art of being present—to God, to people, to the moment.

"The gravitational pull (to hurry) is overwhelming at times. Lately, when that happens, I have this little mantra I repeat:

Slow down. Breathe. Come back to the moment. Receive the good as a gift. Accept the hard as a pathway to peace. Abide."[26]

Notice how Comer is quick to point out that the purpose of these practices is encountering God and abiding in Him. Being with Jesus is always the priority! The practice merely helps us access Him!

⏻ ACTIVATION
Hearing, obeying, and participating with Christ

- What adjustments do you need to make in your way of thinking? Way of living?

- Which of the four spiritual practices do you need to embrace?

- Take a moment and repeat John Mark Comer's mantra:

  Slow down. Breathe. Come back to the moment. Receive the good as a gift. Accept the hard as a pathway to peace. Abide.

Part IV
LIVING FULL

Living Full describes *Christ's life in me* (Colossians 1:27). As a New Covenant disciple of Jesus, I emanate His life everywhere I go! *My authority* in Christ flows from my identity in Christ, while *my power* flows from the fullness of His Spirit living inside me. I am called to be an **ambassador of the Kingdom**, exercising the Father's rule and reign "on earth as it is in heaven" (2 Corinthians 5:20).

MY AUTHORITY IN CHRIST

Therefore, we are ambassadors for Christ, God making his appeal through us. We implore you on behalf of Christ, be reconciled to God (2 Corinthians 5:20 ESV).

MY POWER IN CHRIST

Jesus said . . . you will receive power when the Holy Spirit comes upon you; and you will be my witnesses . . . to the ends of the earth (Acts 1:8).

FIGHTING FROM VICTORY

- When Jesus died and rose again, He defeated death, hell, and the grave. Our responsibility is to agree with this reality.

- Our spiritual journey is accessing our true identity in Christ.

- Satan tries to talk us out of staying engaged with our destiny and original design.

- God designed us to glow with His glory, not walk around depressed and defeated.

- Joy is an inside job; make a decision to be joyful.

- The Cross is where our victory occurs. The Cross is where the enemy's defeat occurs. Therefore, we are no longer fighting for victory; we are fighting from victory!

— Charles Patterson,
Charles Patterson Ministries

16
THE HOLY SPIRIT IN ME
Cultivating Sensitivity to the Spirit

UPWARD

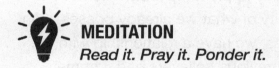

MEDITATION
Read it. Pray it. Ponder it.

> *And don't get drunk with wine, which is rebellion; instead be filled with the fullness of the Holy Spirit (Ephesians 5:18).*

PAUSE AND READ
Ephesians 5:14-18

Understand what it means to live full of the Holy Spirit.

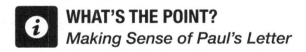

WHAT'S THE POINT?
Making Sense of Paul's Letter

Wake up, sleeper, rise from the dead, and Christ will shine on you (Ephesians 5:14 NIV).

Paul is calling the Ephesian church to wake up to what they already possess! He's saying, "Recognize the light of Christ that is within you and be the light to those around you!" He continues his strong exhortation in Ephesians 5:18:

> And don't get drunk with wine, which is rebellion; instead be filled with the fullness of the Holy Spirit (Ephesians 5:18 NIV).

These verses certainly apply to us today. We need to wake up to the reality of what we already possess. On this side of the cross, we have a relationship with the Holy Spirit that no previous believers had. Let me explain.

DIMENSIONS OF RELATIONSHIP WITH THE HOLY SPIRIT

Paul gave us the key to successful Kingdom-living when he wrote, *"Don't be drunk with wine . . . but be filled with the Holy Spirit"* (Ephesians 5:18). The Greek actually says, *". . . keep on being filled with the Holy Spirit."* (The verb is continuous present tense.) This is of vital importance! We must never neglect this wisdom or take it lightly.

In *Acts*, the disciples and others who were filled with the Spirit at Pentecost are described as *"being filled with the Holy Spirit"* again later in Acts chapter 4 and 7. Being filled with the Spirit was a regular occurrence and should be a normal, daily experience of healthy believers today. As the lamp in the tabernacle (Old Testament) required maintenance to keep burning brightly, so we need to daily walk in union with the Spirit.

There are four kinds of relationships with the Spirit available to ALL people! Scripture describes these four relationships by using four different prepositions: *"with,"* *"in," "upon,"* and *"through."* These relationships with the Spirit of Jesus (Acts 16:7) are progressive. It's vital that you discover which relationship(s) you have, and to continue growing deeper in your "spiritual" life.

"With." Before your conversion, God's Spirit was *with* you, convicting you of your sin of unbelief (John 16:8-9). It was this presence of the Spirit "with" you that inclined you to *repent* (change your way of thinking) and *believe in Jesus* in the first place (Mark 1:15). Jesus said to His disciples in the upper room, *"The Spirit . . . lives 'with' you and will be 'in' you"* (John 14:17).

"In." At the time of your conversion, the Holy Spirit took up residence in you, bringing you into a new relationship. This happened to the apostles after Christ's resurrection when He breathed on them and said, *"Receive the Holy Spirit"* (John 20:22). This experience is called being **born again or born of the Spirit** (John 3:3-8). All true disciples of Jesus have the Spirit living in them (Romans 5:5, 8:9,16; 1 Corinthians 3:16, 6:19-20).

"Upon." Though all true disciples have the Spirit living in them (Romans 8:9), not all are *filled* or *baptized with the Holy Spirit.* The third experience in your relationship with the Spirit is when He comes "upon" you!

Jesus said, *"You will receive power when the Holy Spirit comes 'upon' you . . ."* (Acts 1:8).

Remember, the apostles had already received the Holy Spirit (John 20:22) when this occurred. This *coming upon* is called the **filling** or **baptism in the Holy Spirit!** This relationship *anoints* and *empowers* you for service to Christ and others. It's been said, "The Holy Spirit comes to live inside of us for our benefit, but He fills (baptizes) us for the benefit of the unbelieving world."[27]

"Through." Jesus expresses His endgame in sending His Holy Spirit to live in us.

> . . . *Jesus stood and said in a loud voice, "Let anyone who is thirsty come to me and drink. Whoever believes in me, as Scripture has said, rivers of living water will flow from within them." By this he meant the Spirit, whom those who believed in him were later to receive. Up to that time the Spirit had not been given, since Jesus had not yet been glorified* (John 7:37-39 NIV).

Jesus pointed to the reality that His crucifixion, resurrection, and outpouring of His Spirit would soon bring. Today we live in that reality that Jesus prophesied. As He declared, *". . . rivers of living water will burst out from **within** you, flowing (**through**) you from your innermost being . . ."* (John 7:38, emphasis mine).

The Bible mentions various manifestations of the Spirit. Here's a sampling:

- **Power.** (Acts 1:8)
  This is the manifestation of the baptism (filling) of the Holy Spirit.

- **Speaking in Tongues and Prophesying.** (1 Corinthians 14)
  These are the languages of the Spirit.

- **Boldness.** (Acts 4:31)
  Specifically, boldness in prayer and the proclamation of the Good News.

- **Praising God.** (Acts 10:46)
  This can take an almost infinite number of forms.

- **Gifts of the Spirit.** (1 Corinthians 12)
  Take the time to investigate the nine manifestations of the Spirit listed in 1 Corinthians 12:7-11.

INWARD

GRACE REFLECTIONS
Journaling My Thoughts

1. Share an experience of when you first sensed the Holy Spirit *with* you, wooing you to Jesus.

2. When did you realize your sin of unbelief, repent and wholeheartedly embrace Jesus Christ's forgiveness and salvation? If you've never done this, make today your day of salvation.

3. How can you truly know the Holy Spirit is living *in* you?

4. Have you had a *coming upon/filling/baptism* experience with the Holy Spirit when you received empowering to do the works of Christ (John 14:12; Acts 1:8)?

5. What are some fresh baptisms (empowering revelations) of the Holy Spirit you have received since your initial baptism of the Spirit (i.e., baptism of love, baptism of innocence)?

6. What are some ways the Spirit flows *through* you like rivers of living water? What are some of the manifestations of the Holy Spirit that you experience regularly?

OUTWARD

LIVING FULL
Cultivating Sensitivity to the Spirit

The two particular ways that God reveals Himself to us are in His *transcendence and immanence.* Transcendence is the aspect of God's nature and power that is wholly independent of the material universe, beyond all known physical laws. Immanence is where God is fully present in the physical world and thus fully accessible.

Brother Lawrence, a lay brother in a Carmelite monastery in Paris in the 1600s, referred to his intimate, moment-by-moment relationship with the Holy Spirit as "practicing the presence of God." He understood that his union with God was *immanent* and continually accessible.

In the 21st century, Pastor Bill Johnson has popularized the practice of "hosting the presence of God." Both of these men have written books that are helpful tools for cultivating sensitivity to the Holy Spirit. Brother Lawrence's book, *The Practice of the Presence,* was compiled after his death. Bill Johnson's current book is *Hosting the Presence.* I highly recommend each of these spiritual classics.

Often the Holy Spirit manifests Himself powerfully during corporate times of worship. He *comes upon* us in an extraordinary and transcendent manner. But most often, personal worship is cultivating sensitivity to our *always indwelling* Holy Spirit. This is an intimate and immanent relationship with God that is always accessible.

The truth is, Jesus exists in heavenly places (realms) and on earth simultaneously. But hold on, so do you and I. Listen to Paul's explanation in Ephesians 2:6 (NIV):

> *And God raised us up with Christ and seated us with him in the heavenly realms in Christ Jesus . . .*

The Passion Translation amplifies this verse saying,

">. . . we ascended with him into the glorious perfection and authority of the heavenly realm, for we are now co-seated as one with Christ!"*

So, our responsibility is now to become sensitive to the activity of Holy Spirit *within* and *from heavenly realms.* Our immanent relationship with Holy Spirit is expressed by His living "in" and "through" us. Our transcendent relationship with Holy Spirit is experienced when He manifests "upon" us.

We must create space to cultivate sensitivity to Holy Spirit and host His presence.

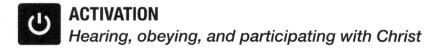

ACTIVATION
Hearing, obeying, and participating with Christ

- **What is God saying to you?**

- What adjustments do you need to make to create space to cultivate sensitivity to Holy Spirit?

- With whom do you think this would be beneficial to share?

17
SPIRIT-FILLED FAMILY
Bridal Love

UPWARD

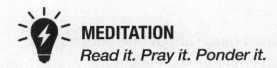

MEDITATION
Read it. Pray it. Ponder it.

Submit to one another out of reverence for
Christ (Ephesians 5:21 NIV).

PAUSE AND READ
Ephesians 5:17-6:4

Understand what a Spirit-filled family looks like.

WHAT'S THE POINT?
Making Sense of Paul's Letter

I met my wife, Lesa, as a 20-year-old student at
Southwest Texas State University. We were married at
the age of 22 *on the actual day* of my graduation. Clearly,
we were eager to be married and begin our new life
together.

Now, after 36 years of marriage, four sons, three daughters-in-law, a grandson and five different ministry assignments along the way, we find ourselves back where we started—in San Marcos, Texas. Much has changed. The college is now called Texas State University, and the student population is more than twice the size it was when we were students. Along with the growth of the school, the entire region has exploded with growth.

Lesa and I have learned much about one another over the years, but perhaps the biggest lesson has come from Ephesians 5:21 (NIV): *"Submit to one another out of reverence for Christ."* Submitting means putting others before yourself; it means not always doing what you want to do. It means putting God's desires above your own desires.

The truth is, Lesa could never submit to me based on my "track record." I've blown it many times over 36 years. But that's not what the Scripture says. Again, Ephesians 5:21 says, *"Submit to one another **out of reverence for Christ**."* And because we are both indwelled with the Spirit of Jesus, it's easy for me to submit to the Christ *in* Lesa and for Lesa to submit to the Christ *in* me.

Submission in marriage always begins with *mutual submission* to Christ. Husbands and wives should act and interact around this sure foundation. Jesus Christ is the head of the marriage and the ultimate leader and authority.

Paul compares marriage to the connection between Christ and the Church. The relationship isn't that of a master to a servant; it's that of lover to his/her beloved.

SPIRIT-FILLED FAMILY

The Spirit-filled family has always been God's plan for families! Notice Ephesians 5:18-20 (NIV):

> Do not be drunk on wine . . . Instead, be filled with the Spirit, speaking to one another with psalms, hymns, and songs from the Spirit. Sing and make music from your heart to the Lord, always giving thanks to God the Father for everything, in the name of our Lord Jesus Christ.

This is what a Spirit-filled family looks like:

- They sing songs together in the Spirit.

- They share what they're grateful for around the dinner table—while playing games, having a picnic, or just doing life together.

- They are a joyful family that intentionally creates an atmosphere of thanksgiving for each person's oneness with Father in Christ by the power of the Holy Spirit.

How does a *husband* mutually submit to his wife?

A husband willingly lays down his life for his wife in the same way Jesus gave His life for the life of His bride. A husband is not a tyrant who forces or coerces his wife to submit to his selfish desires. No, *he submits to his wife's need to feel loved, cared for, served, protected, led, and secured.* He demonstrates love with the same tender devotion that Christ demonstrated to us, His bride (Ephesians 5:25-33).

How does a *wife* submit to her husband?

A wife is to submit to her husband in the same way she is tenderly devoted to the Lord (Ephesians 5:22, 24). When people in Western society read these verses, many get frustrated because they perceive this passage as being demeaning to women and lessening their worth. This is not the intention at all. Submission in marriage is *the heart of respect* a wife has for her husband. Submit (*be devoted, respect, support* as sometimes translated) is not something degrading or humiliating. It doesn't mean wives are to be a "doormat" or have no opinions of their own. No, submission carries the idea that the heart of the wife is to be *supportive of her husband*. She does so of free choice, and in choosing to support her husband, she is empowering him to have the self-respect that he needs to be the man she needs.

It's really a reciprocation of honor (empathetic support, give and take) that Paul is conveying. Husbands *love their wives* so their wives can be all they were created to be. Wives *respect their husbands* so their husbands can be all God created them to be. This is the foundation of a harmonious, Spirit-filled family.

How should children respond to their parents?

> *Children, if you want to be wise, listen to your parents and do what they tell you, and the Lord will help you. For the commandment, "Honor your father and your mother," was the first of the Ten Commandments with a promise attached: "You will prosper and live a long, full life if you honor your parents"* (Ephesians 5:1-2 TPT).

I don't think this needs much explanation! Kids listen to your parents. Honor your father and mother. This will create the foundation for a long and full life.

How should fathers respond to their children?

> *Fathers, don't exasperate your children, but raise them up with loving discipline and counsel that brings the revelation of our Lord* (Ephesians 5:4).

Patience is a fruit of the Spirit. As a father of four sons, I'm sure I have exasperated my boys at times. We frustrate our children when we don't take the necessary time to listen well, explain thoroughly, show them "how," and walk with them. Raising up children takes intentionality, time and patience. I promise you it's worth the investment.

Did you notice the phrase "counsel that brings the revelation of our Lord" (Ephesians 5:4)? That phrase is the key to Better Covenant parenting. We are to raise sons and daughters who can receive the New Covenant revelation (unveiling) of *our* Lord. That's the goal, not coercing them to do what we want *or else*.

INWARD

GRACE REFLECTIONS
Journaling My Thoughts

1. What does "submit to one another out of reverence for Christ" look like to you personally?

2. Is your family a Spirit-filled family? What dynamics would need to change in order for this to occur? What's your part (Ephesians 5:18-20)?

3. How does a *husband* mutually submit to his wife? Is this idea new to you?

4. How does a *wife* submit to her husband?

5. How did you respond to your parents when you were a child? Do you (plan to) parent differently than your parents?

6. Why do you think Paul addressed fathers but not mothers in regard to parenting?

OUTWARD

LIVING FULL
Bridal Love

The primary way of picturing relationship with God and Israel in the Old Testament is through using the metaphor of *marriage.* Paul uses the bridal theme in Ephesians 5 to describe Jesus' relationship with His Church.

In the Old Testament, Yahweh was always trying to woo Israel back from her idolatrous relationship with other gods. The imagery of Yahweh as Israel's husband runs throughout: Isaiah 54; Jeremiah 3, 31; Ezekiel 16; etc.

Can you imagine having the prophetic calling that Hosea had? God told him to marry a prostitute named Gomer and have children with her (Hosea 1-3). After the marriage, she did not quit her "day job," as she continued her promiscuous and adulterous ways. Yet, God told Hosea to pursue his wayward harlot wife.

Hosea 3:1 tells us "she is loved by another man and is an adulteress." God instructs Hosea to buy Gomer back, and he does. In essence, it appears that Hosea buys his own wife on the auction block to salvage her from human sex slavery.

This is the picture of Yahweh's great love for His wayward people. Comparing Himself to a husband whose wife has committed adultery, Yahweh is patient and sacrificial beyond comprehension. Ultimately, with the death of His Son (Jesus), Yahweh redeems His lost bride from her self-destruction to live a life of love, freedom, and fullness in Christ.

The New Testament depicts Jesus as the heavenly bridegroom Who came to earth in search of a bride (Matthew 9:15, 25:1-13; John 3:29). The book of Revelation depicts the Church as the "Bride of Christ" at a wedding festival (Revelation 19,21,22). Throughout the New Testament, the Church is portrayed as all who've entered into a New Covenant bridal relationship with Jesus.

The whole point of salvation is that it's all about a Marriage! Gregg Boyd declares:

> The good news is that God wants a marriage covenant with us—His whole life poured out for us . . . our whole life poured out for Him.

> The good news is that Jesus came as the Bridegroom to rescue His Bride from her self-imprisonment to satan, idolatry, and wrong thinking.

> The Cross is God's marriage proposal: This is what you mean to Me, this is how valuable you are to Me, will you marry Me?[28]

ACTIVATION
Hearing, obeying, and participating with Christ

- **Have you accepted God's marriage proposal at the cross?**

- What is the first adjustment you will need to make in order to have a Spirit-filled family?

18
BECAUSE I BELONG TO JESUS... I AM VICTORIOUS

Weapons of Our Warfare

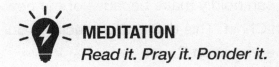

MEDITATION
Read it. Pray it. Ponder it.

> *Finally, be strong in the Lord and in his mighty power. Put on the full armor of God, so that you can take your stand against the devil's schemes. For our struggle is not against flesh and blood, but against the rulers, against the authorities, against the powers of this dark world and against the spiritual forces of evil in the heavenly realms (Ephesians 6:10-12 NIV).*

PAUSE AND READ
Ephesians 6:10-20

Understand the full armor of God and its usage.

ℹ️ WHAT'S THE POINT?
Making Sense of Paul's Letter

Ephesians 6:10-20 is Paul's summary of his letter. He masterfully weaves the magnificent themes of Ephesians into the familiar picture of a Roman soldier's armor. Take a moment to read it.

I have taken the truths of this brilliant passage and turned them into a *Better Covenant declaration.* This is a declaration that we can boldly make because of our new identity and union in Christ. This declaration declares our spiritual power and authority in Christ.

I believe the declaration as written below, titled "Because I Belong to Jesus," captures the reason Paul wrote *Ephesians.*

Because I belong to Jesus, I have all the right equipment to stand against the enemy.

Because of the cross, the resurrection, the ascension, and the forever enthronement of King Jesus—I stand in a place of victory!

Because of King Jesus, my daily battles are *from* a position of victory, not *for* victory!

Because I belong to Jesus, I am equipped with the *belt of truth*. The primary power of the Gospel of the Kingdom is that *it is true!*

I declare that the Gospel works because the Gospel is True! It has full effect every time it goes forth. The Gospel is the Way, the Truth and the Life. Jesus is the Gospel! Jesus is *Truth*!

The *belt of truth* dispels all the lies of the enemy! It holds everything together and in its proper place.

Because I belong to Jesus, I am equipped with the *breastplate of righteousness*. My identity is in Jesus, and I am now the righteousness of God in Christ Jesus.

I declare that I am no longer a slave to sin, shame, guilt, or fear—I am a child of God! I am a new creation! I am the righteousness of God!

I declare that my heart, my emotions, my affections, and my desires are protected by the *breastplate of righteousness*.

I declare that I am free from striving, free from the performance game and the approval trap. I'm now free to relax and rest in the finished work of Jesus!

Because I belong to Jesus, I am equipped with the *Gospel of peace shoes*.

I declare that the peace and forgiveness of Jesus, the Lamb, has forever conquered the violence and judgment of the beasts of darkness!

I declare that Jesus is my peace! He has destroyed the dividing wall of the Law with its commands and regulations. He has created in Himself *one new humanity* by the Gospel of peace!

I choose to hold fast to Christ's *Gospel of peace* and boldly declare—"Mercy always triumphs over judgment, and Love always wins!"

Because I belong to Jesus, I am equipped with the *shield of faith!*

I declare my loyalty to Jesus, my risen Lord. I declare that He will protect me when the enemy hurls flaming arrows at me.

In Jesus' name, I renounce the arrows of *doubt, discouragement,* and *temptation!*

I renounce *shame, fear, guilt,* and *unbelief.*

I declare that my trust and dependence in Jesus will quench every fiery arrow of the enemy! I declare that I will not be robbed of faith, hope, joy, or love.

Because I belong to Jesus, I am equipped with the *helmet of salvation.*

I declare that my mind is protected from the lies and accusations of the enemy. I have been rescued from satan and now face all secondary enemies with the mind of Christ who lives in me!

Because I belong to Jesus, I am equipped with the *sword of the Spirit*, which is the *Word of God!*

I declare that the living Word of God is active and penetrating through the person of Jesus, Who lives within me.

I declare that I have received the living and written *sword of the Spirit* to kill any demonic giant in my life.

I will use the *Word of God* as a standard to weigh and challenge all of my life experiences.

Today, I kill the giant of *discouragement* with the *Word of God* in my mouth.

Today, I kill the giant of *hopelessness* through the *Word of God* in my mouth.

Today, I kill the giants of *false identity*, *unbelief*, *distrust, and striving*—in Jesus' name!

Because I am in union with Jesus and His Spirit lives in me, I will fearlessly *pray in the Spirit* on all occasions, with all kinds of prayers and requests, for all the Lord's people.

I declare blessing on the Church of my city and region. Awaken us to the reality that we have already been blessed with every spiritual blessing in King Jesus.

I declare the Church of my city and region is a beautiful Bride of Christ, a united and healthy Body of Jesus, and the all-welcoming Family of God. We are a tangible expression of heaven invading earth with the glory of God!

Because I belong to Jesus, I will *live loved, live full,* and *live free!*

INWARD

GRACE REFLECTIONS
Journaling My Thoughts

1. Which of the points of declaration most resonate with you in this season of your life?

2. How will believing that the Cross is where our *victory* occurred change the way you live each day?

3. How will believing that the Cross is where the enemy's *defeat* occurred change the way you live each day?

4. How will believing that we are no longer fighting *for* victory, but rather *from* a place of victory change the way you live each day?

5. **Which giants do you need to slay** *(i.e. hopelessness, false identity, unbelief, distrust, striving, fear, shame, condemnation, separation, anger, ingratitude, criticism, etc.)***? Explain.**

OUTWARD

  LIVING FULL & FREE
Weapons of our Warfare

In 2 Corinthians 10:3-5 (NIV), Paul writes . . .

For though we live in the world, we do not wage war as the world does. The weapons we fight with are not the weapons of the world. On the contrary, they have divine power to demolish strongholds. We demolish arguments and every pretension that sets itself up against the knowledge of God, and we take captive every thought to make it obedient to Christ.

Bad news: We are in a war (v. 3)!

Good News: We have powerful God-weapons (v. 4).

Bad news: Barriers are being built against Truth (v. 4).

Good News: Every one of our loose thoughts, emotions, impulses, and attitudes can be taken "captive" like prisoners of war (v. 5).

The Passion Translation renders v. 6 this way:

> *Since we are armed with such dynamic weaponry, we stand ready to punish any trace of rebellion, as soon as you choose complete obedience.*

Obedience is our choice that accesses the victory of God's grace!

A stronghold (v.4) is an area of weakness where you have believed a lie, and therefore have given satan access to your life. Strongholds are "houses of thoughts." Francis Frangipane expounds, "A stronghold is a mindset impregnated with hopelessness that causes us to accept as unchangeable something that we know is contrary to the will and word of God."

Strongholds begin in the mind as a *thought.* They soon become an *imagination,* an intent to do the thing you have been thinking. In time, the result of thoughts that come to reality is a full-grown *stronghold.*

There are three arenas of strongholds:

- Individual thoughts (Ephesians 2:2-3).

- Thought systems, philosophies, political ideologies, and world religion beliefs (Colossians 2:8).

- Geographic and political (Daniel 10:13).

Strongholds topple when we *recognize* them, *repent* and *realign* with Jesus, *renounce* the lie behind it, and *receive* the empowering presence of God's Spirit (grace).

Offensive weapons of our spiritual warfare[29] include the following:

- Word (Ephesians 6:17).

- Blood covenant (Revelation 12:11).

- Testimony of Jesus (Revelation 12:11).

- Name of Jesus, our power of attorney (Acts 2:38, 3:6).

Defensive weapons of our spiritual warfare include the following:

- Truth (Ephesians 6:14).

- Righteousness (Ephesians 6:14).

- Peace (Ephesians 6:15).

- Faith (Ephesians 6:16).

- Salvation (Ephesians 6:17).

Launching Rockets (which all come from the mouth):

- Prayer

- Praise and Worship

- Preaching and Teaching

- Testimony

⏻ ACTIVATION
Hearing, obeying, and participating with Christ

- What offensive and defensive weapons of warfare are you currently utilizing? *(See pages 251-252.)*

- What *Launching Rockets* do you utilize most? Explain. *(See page 252.)*

- On what sin pattern, thought pattern or emotional **stronghold** is the Holy Spirit putting His finger?

- What is the lie you are hearing in your head?

- What is the *scriptural truth* that needs to be applied?

- Where do you need to *repent, grant forgiveness* or *renounce* a particular stronghold?

19
LIVING LOVED, FULL AND FREE

Kingdom Living

UPWARD

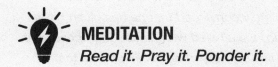

MEDITATION

Read it. Pray it. Ponder it.

> *Therefore if anyone is in Christ, he is a new creature; the old things passed away; behold, new things have come (2 Corinthians 5:17 NASB).*

PAUSE AND READ

2 Corinthians 5:14-6:2

Understand the heart and soul of Kingdom-living.

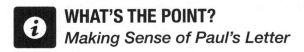 **WHAT'S THE POINT?**
Making Sense of Paul's Letter

I love 2 Corinthians 5:14-6:2. Over the years, I have probably preached more messages from this passage than any other in Scripture. Why? Because this passage succinctly describes what it means to be a Better Covenant disciple, living on the right side of the cross. It resonates with the heart and soul of Kingdom-living.

Here's a quick synopsis:

- **We are *compelled* by Jesus' once-for-all death and resurrection.**

  "It is Christ's love that fuels our passion and motivates us, because we are absolutely convinced that he has given his life for all of us. This means we all died with him so that those who live should no longer live self-absorbed lives but lives that are poured out for him—the one who died for us and now lives again" (vv. 14-15 TPT).

- **Anyone who is in union with Christ is a new creation with a New Covenant identity.** The old man and the Old Covenant have passed away; everything is fresh and new (vv. 16-17).

- **God in Christ reconciled the world (cosmos) to Himself on the cross and has now committed to believers the message of reconciliation.** This is the Good News of the Kingdom of God (vv. 18-19).

- **We have been empowered and authorized as Christ's ambassadors to spread the message of reconciliation and ministry of the Kingdom of heaven here on planet Earth.** Did you get that? Our Kingdom calling is to be re-presentatives of Christ. Our Kingdom message is the message of reconciliation (v. 20).

- **Reconciliation carries the idea of "restoration to oneness."** Oneness was always God's intention for humanity: oneness with Himself in His Divine Dance and oneness with each other. Mankind's original identity was lost (stolen) through agreement with a lie perpetuated by satan, but in time that intended identity was restored by Jesus' death and resurrection. **Today, our true identity in Christ is the righteousness of God through our union with Jesus** (v. 21).

- **"Now is the time of God's favor; now is the day of salvation."** Today, all believers live on the right side of the cross and have a restored and empowered identity in Christ (2 Corinthians 6:2). That's Good News worth sharing.

INWARD

GRACE REFLECTIONS
Journaling My Thoughts

1. There are three primary motivators: *fear, incentive,* and *love.*

   What's your motivation for being a disciple and for making disciples of Jesus? Explain.

2. The idea of being a "new creation" is actually the idea of being a new, Spirit-indwelled species. Do you see your new union and identity in Christ this way? Explain.

II Corinthians 5:19 says, "God was reconciling the world to himself in Christ, not counting people's sins against them. And he has committed to us the message of reconciliation." Can you imagine? We are **pre-forgiven** because of Jesus' once-for-all death and resurrection. All that remains is for the drawing work of the Holy Spirit and the obedience of Spirit-indwelled believers to share this Good News!

3. How does the idea of "pre-forgiveness" at the cross in AD 30 change the way you evangelize others with the message of reconciliation?

Reconciliation is an interesting word, full of rich meaning.
Re = "to go back"; *concile* = "to make one."
Reconciliation is *going back to the garden and God's original purpose of covenant oneness with mankind.*
Another definition of reconciliation is *friendship restored!*

4. What does the word *reconciliation* mean to you personally?

5. What does being an ambassador of Christ look like for you?

OUTWARD

KINGDOM-LIVING
How to Bear Fruit

As the New Year began, I asked, "Lord, what's on Your heart?" I felt this distinct impression: "I (the Lord) am going to give you a new lens through which to evaluate success. I am giving you a Kingdom lens!"

I learned that a Kingdom lens is made up of three parts: *the priority, the assignment* and *the fruit.* The Lord made it clear that the order was critical. *The priority* was of utmost importance. *The assignment* would flow from the priority, and *the fruit* would overflow from the assignment. This is the way of the Kingdom of God.

THE PRIORITY
Matthew 11:28-30

The root word of priority is *prior,* which means "before." Therefore, the equation for determining one's priority looks like this: "Nothing comes before _____." The Lord spoke clearly that He desired my blank to be filled with the word REST!

Rest? Are you sure that's the right word? That is perhaps the last word I would have chosen.

What follows is what I've been learning about the counterintuitive way of Jesus and His Kingdom.

> *Then Jesus exclaimed, "Father, thank you, for you are Lord, the Supreme Ruler over heaven and earth! And you have hidden the great revelation of your authority from those who are proud and wise in their own eyes. Instead, you have shared it with these who humble themselves. Yes, Father, your plan delights your heart, as you've chosen this way to extend your kingdom—by giving it to those who have become like trusting children. You have entrusted me with all that you are and all that you have. No one fully and intimately knows the Son except the Father. And no one fully and intimately knows the Father except the Son. But the Son is able to unveil the Father to anyone he chooses.*

> *"Are you weary, carrying a heavy burden? Then come to me. I will refresh your life, for I am your oasis. Simply join your life with mine. Learn my ways and you'll discover that I'm gentle, humble, easy to please. **You will find refreshment and rest in me.** For all that I require of you will be pleasant and easy to bear* (Matthew 11:25-30 TPT).

Rest is a difficult concept for us busy Westerners to grasp because it requires the ruthless elimination of hurry![30] On the seventh day, the day after His creation of man, God rested. Interestingly, man's first day after being created began with rest.

Man was created to work from a place of rest, not rest because he was so exhausted from work. The idea of rest is "sitting with God." We are to start each work week from a place of abiding rest. In fact, Jesus said, ". . . He who abides in Me, and I in him, bears much fruit; for without Me you can do nothing" (John 15:5 NKJV).

Abiding-rest cultivates sensitivity to the Spirit of Jesus within. Abiding with Jesus is hosting the Presence of God. It is experiencing deep communion with the One with whom you are in union.

We must learn to abide in Christ. Our choice to abide ("sit with Christ") requires humility and faith. Abiding opens the door of our soul to the flow of the Spirit. On the other hand, our pride and unbelief keep the door of the Spirit's life-flow closed!

As we abide in Christ, we experience His life flowing through us, which results in bearing fruit quite naturally without self-effort and striving.

THE ASSIGNMENT
Matthew 6:33

The Church is a Kingdom family. The Kingdom of God is a family business: *relational, revelational,* and *generational.* Therefore, we are a family on mission to represent our Father and His family (Ephesians 3:14-15).

As a member of God's Kingdom family, our assignment is to give our full attention to Kingdom-living.

For better or worse, we become what we give our attention to. Attention leads to awareness. Do you want to be more aware of God and the ways of His Kingdom? It will require you to *slow down* and give Father your attention. Hurry kills all we hold dear: *spiritual awareness, health, marriage, family, creativity, generosity, gratitude, _____.* You fill in the blank.

Pastor Jimmy Seibert gives five spheres of relationship that comprise our Kingdom assignment. I've adapted them for our purposes:

1. **Our life in Christ.** This is our abiding relationship in union with Jesus (John 14:20).

2. **Life-on-life relationships.** These are "garden friends." Those who stick with you through thick and thin. Jesus had three disciples (Peter, James, and John) who were with Him in the Garden of Gethsemane. These are deeply committed friends with whom you process life.

3. **Spiritual family.** Jesus had twelve male disciples who did life with Him. He also had a group of women disciples who supported Him.

4. **Larger family (reunion).** In the West, we typically call this larger weekly gathering "church." In truth, this gathering is more like halftime at a football game. It's a time for the team (family) to rest, review, re-set, refocus, and return back to the game on Monday morning, carrying fresh Kingdom revelation, strength, and encouragement. As royal priests (1 Peter 2:9), we minister to the heart of the Lord in the "gathering," and we minister from the heart of the Lord wherever we go . . .

5. **Friends, family, co-workers, classmates, neighbors, divine encounters, etc.** Have you ever prayed, "Father, I give you permission to interrupt my day"? I promise He will take you up on that prayer. Have you ever gotten mad or frustrated when your schedule was thrown off course by unwanted interruption, and then realized it was because you asked God to "interrupt" your day? God delights to take us out of our comfort zone to bring people our way who need what we have— Jesus and His Kingdom. Why? Because we are a family on mission to represent our Father and His family. It's our Kingdom assignment.

THE FRUIT
John 15:5

A Kingdom lens is a very different way to see what matters most in life. It's a different metric to measure "success."

Fruit is the overflow of "excess life." In Jesus' famous teaching in John 15, His whole point is that we cannot produce fruit on our own. Fruit is the product of a branch (me) being in union with the vine (Jesus). The sap (life) in the vine trunk flows out to the connected branch and then overflows with excess life, which is called fruit.

If we get the priority right—fruit will come (John 15:5).

If we are faithful in stewarding our assignment—fruit will be produced (Matthew 6:33).

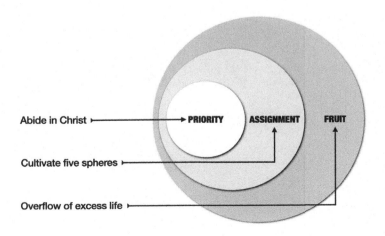

⏻ ACTIVATION
Hearing, obeying, and participating with Christ

- Go over each of your five spheres of relationship. Where is God inviting you to participate with Him?

- Where will you begin in eliminating hurry and busyness so you can give greater attention to God?

How to
LIVE LOVED **EACH DAY**

To begin this book I shared seven Kingdom realities that have shaped my life. To conclude, it only seems right to share the seven Better Covenant realities in *Living Loved* that have become my daily pillars.

I exhort you to meditate on these seven realities each day. They will provide much needed perspective and encouragement for your daily spiritual journey.

1. God's **GRACE** is His empowering presence that enables me to be who God created me to be. His grace is sufficient for everything I will encounter today.

2. My **UNION** with Christ is the source of every good work that flows through me.

3. My **IDENTITY** flows from the reality of who I am in Christ. I am confident and secure because of my oneness with Christ.

4. Each **MYSTERY** I encounter is an invitation to greater intimacy with God—which will result in greater revelation.

5. My **PURITY** is the fruit of Christ's life flowing through me. My holiness comes from the Holy Spirit who lives in me. I am the righteousness of God and fully innocent in Christ. Therefore, I can live full and free. My past shame, guilt and fear are "finished"!

6. My **AUTHORITY** flows from embracing my union, identity and purity in Christ. As a son/daughter of God, I am authorized and empowered to emanate His glory everywhere I go.

7. **I RE-PRESENT** what God is truly like to every person I encounter. As an ambassador of Jesus Christ, I best re-present (Father-Son-Spirit) when I am living loved, living full and living free!

WHO I AM IN CHRIST[31]

There is absolutely nothing more securing than knowing the truth about who God truly is and who the Bible says I am in Christ. Regularly making these declarations of your identity in Christ will build your faith and enable you to live more confidently and powerfully—the way you were intended to live.

- **I AM** made in the image and likeness of God (*Genesis 1:26*).

- **I AM** a child of God, skillfully, wonderfully and marvelously made *(John 1:12; Psalm 139:14-18)*.

- **I AM** God's child, for I am born again of the incorruptible seed of the Word of God which lives and abides forever *(1 Peter 1:23)*.

- **I AM** forgiven all my sins and washed in the blood of Jesus *(Ephesians 1:7; Hebrews 9:14: Colossians 1:14; 1 John 2:12)*.

- **I AM** loved, precious, forgiven, cleansed, valuable and His delight *(1 John 1:9, 3:1, 4:19; Psalm 16:3)*.

- **I AM** created for great things that God has prepared for me *(Ephesians 2:10, 3:20; 1 Corinthians 2:12)*.

- **I AM** a new creation, old things have passed away, all things have been made new *(2 Corinthians 5:17)*.

- **I AM** sanctified, chosen, made holy, righteous and pure *(1 Corinthians 6:11; 2 Corinthians 5:21; Colossians 3:12)*.

- **I AM** saved by grace through faith so all His promises are mine *(Ephesians 2:8; Galatians 3:2-5; Romans 4:16-21)*.

- **I AM** justified (declared innocent) freely by grace—I now enjoy peace with God *(Romans 3:24, 28; 5:1)*.

- **I AM** chosen by God— a royal priest, holy and set apart as His *(John 15:16; 1 Peter 2:9)*.

- **I AM** a king and a priest, and rule and reign in life *(Revelation 1:6, 5:1; Romans 5:17)*.

- **I AM** victorious every day by the greater one that is in me *(1 Corinthians 15:57; 1 John 4:4, 5:4)*.

- **I AM** delivered from the powers of darkness *(1 Peter 2:9; Colossians 1:13-14, 2:12)*.

- **I AM** redeemed from the curse of the law and the devil's power is destroyed *(Galatians 3:13; 1 John 3:8)*.

- **I HAVE** been given authority over the enemy and he is under my feet *(Luke 10:19; Ephesians 1:22, 3:10; Hebrews 2:8)*.

- **I AM** anointed, directed and hear God's voice *(1 John 2:20,27; John 10:4,16, 27; Romans 8:14; Psalms 37:23)*.

- **I AM** God's son/daughter and a citizen of heaven *(Romans 8:14,16; Philippians 3:20).*

- **I AM** an heir of God and a joint heir with Jesus— I have been blessed in the heavenly realms with every spiritual blessing in Christ *(Romans 8:17; Colossians 1:12; Ephesians 1:3).*

- **I AM** a partaker of God's divine nature and have been given all things *(2 Peter 1:3-4).*

- **I AM** an heir of eternal life, and my eternal life has already started *(1 John 5:11-12; Ephesians 1:4, 11; John 17:3).*

- **I AM** kept safely and surrounded by angels—so I am never afraid *(Psalm 91:11; Hebrew 1:14; Joshua 1:9).*

- **I AM** strong in the Lord's power and His joy is my strength *(Ephesians 6:10; Nehemiah 8:10).*

- **I AM** doing all things in Christ because all things are possible in Christ *(Philippians 4:13; Mark 9:23).*

- **I AM** casting all my cares on the Lord and worry about nothing *(Philippians 4:6; 1 Peter 5:7).*

- **I AM** getting all my needs met by Jesus as He abundantly supplies *(Philippians 4:19; 2 Corinthians 8:9).*

- **I AM** blessed with all spiritual and natural blessings, everything I'll ever need *(Ephesians 1:3; 2 Peter 1:3).*

- **I AM** reaping rewards and increase and freely giving because I am already blessed *(Galatians 6:9: 2 Corinthians 9:6-11).*

- **I AM** healed by the stripes of Jesus— He took all of my sickness *(1 Peter 2:24; Matthew 8:17; Acts 10:38; Psalm 103:3).*

- **I AM** not moved by what I see, I walk by faith not by sight *(2 Corinthians 4:18, 5:7).*

- **I AM** more than a conqueror and victorious in all things *(Romans 8:37; 1 Corinthians 15:57).*

- **I AM** a bold overcomer by the blood of the lamb and the word of my testimony *(Revelation 12:11; 1 John 5:4-5).*

- **I AM** the temple of the Holy Spirit and anointed with power *(1 Corinthians 3:16, 6:19; 1 John 2:20, 27; Acts 1:8)*.

- **I AM** the light of the world, establishing God's way, truth and life here on earth *(Matthew 5:14, 16:19, 28:19-20)*.

- **I AM** moving from glory to glory, transformed into His image by His Spirit in me *(2 Corinthians 3:18)*.

- **I AM** united together with Christ, being one Spirit with Him *(1 Corinthians 6:17; Romans 6:5, 8:11)*.

- **I AM** in union and oneness with Christ—I in Him and He in me *(John 17:23; Galatians 2:20; Ephesians 2:6; 1 John 4:17)*.

- **I AM** filled with the Spirit of Christ to do the works He did— and even greater! *(John 14:12)*.

- **I AM** a laborer together with God— at complete rest, ease and no striving *(2 Corinthians 6:1; Matthew 11:28-30; Hebrews 4:10)*.

- **I AM** filled and flooded with God—I His power, love and ability flow through me *(Ephesians 1:19, 3:19-20; 2 Corinthians 3:4-5).*

- **I AM** Jesus Christ's ambassador on planet earth, sharing His good news of reconciliation *(2 Corinthians 5:20).*

- **I AM** a member of the body of Christ— His hands, His feet, and His voice in the earth *(1 Corinthians 12:27, 14:3, 31; Mark 16:15-20).*

- **I AM** always in His presence, in His glory, filled with JOY *(Matthew 28:20; Psalm 139:7; Acts 2:28)!*

A1
WAYS TO APPROACH THIS BOOK
Appendix

Personal study. Read from start to finish as an individual study to build a firm spiritual foundation.

Mentoring/Discipling relationships. Use for a spiritual parenting relationship or a group of "two or three," giving mutual care to each other.

- **BACK** - Provides a time for mutual care, encouragement, and "yay, God!" stories.

- **UP** - Focuses on mutual discovery from the Scripture.

- **IN** - Focuses on authentic sharing from *Grace Reflections* and processing life together.

- **OUT** - Casts vision for ways to "live out" and share what you are learning.

Small group study. This is similar to discipling/ mentoring groups except the group is larger and may incorporate more teaching.

I encourage dialogue with a friend or small group. I truly believe that it's in the soil of authentic community that our personal spirituality comes alive and grows best.

—Larry Kreider

A2
WHY CHOOSE
THE PASSION TRANSLATION?
Appendix

STEVE'S THOUGHTS

Perhaps you are not familiar with *The Passion Translation.* For this reason, I am taking a moment to explain why I have chosen this particular translation for the majority of this book.

- Each translation of the Bible chooses a particular nuance to highlight. *The Passion Translation* of *Ephesians* uses language that highlights Paul's focus on our identity in Christ, our union in Christ, our unity with the Body of Christ, and our authority in Christ.

- *The Passion Translation* has a wonderful conversational cadence and flow that makes it easy to read and understand the main message the author is trying to communicate.

- Often familiar translations can cause some to go on "autopilot" while reading overfamiliar passages. I believe it is a sin to allow Holy Scripture to lose its flavor and become bland or boring. My heart is to help you fall in love with the Bible. This requires language that resonates with your mind and heart.

- *The Passion Translation* speaks the language that passionate people understand. *TPT* brings the heart and soul of Scripture alive in a fresh and vibrant way that inspires believers to actually live a Better Covenant life!

- The purpose of Better Covenant discipleship is to activate disciples of Jesus to be who God created them to be and to re-present what God is truly like. *The Passion Translation* is written in a manner that activates individuals to be "doers of the word and not hearers only."

TPT EDITOR'S THOUGHTS
From ThePassionTranslation.Com

The Passion Translation's goal is to bring God's fiery heart of love and truth to this generation, merging the emotion and truth of God's Word, resulting in a clear, accurate, readable translation for modern English readers.

The Passion Translation's **philosophy** is that the meaning of God's original message to the world has priority over its exact form, which is why the goal is to communicate the meaning of the Scripture as clearly and naturally as possible in modern English. The TPT has sought to remain faithful to the original biblical languages by preserving their literal meaning, yet remain flexible enough to convey God's original message in a way modern English speakers can clearly understand and encounter the heart of God through the message of truth and love.

COMPARING *THE PASSION TRANSLATION* WITH OTHERS

The basic kinds of Bible translations are *formal* equivalence and *functional* equivalence.

Formal **equivalence describes the** *literal word-for-word versions* (i.e., KJV, ESV). Formal equivalence believes the **"literal meaning" should have priority**, that the Hebrew and Greek words should equal English ones.

Functional **or** *dynamic* **equivalence describes thought-for-thought versions** (i.e., New Century Version, NLT). Functional equivalence believes the **"original message" should have priority**, that what

God was trying to communicate through Hebrew and Greek should be what is communicated in English.

TPT is a balanced translation that tries to hold both the Word's literal meaning and original message in proper tension.

STEVE'S FINAL THOUGHTS

Though I have chosen to use *The Passion Translation* as the primary translation for this book, I must confess that I am a "word" guy. I love to study the nuanced meaning of words. I regularly read literal word-for-word translations in order to have a more precise understanding of the meaning and historical context of various words and idioms.

The issue of Bible translation is not an "either/or" proposition; it's "both/and." Therefore, I highly recommend that you use various *word-for-word* translations and a good Greek and Hebrew interlinear Bible to accompany this study through *Ephesians*. This will provide a much more textured reading of the passages that are covered in *Living Loved.*

THANKS

Nothing in life is successful without the combined effort of many gifted people who are willing to contribute their time, talent, and passion for a common goal. I am grateful for those who helped make this book a reality:

- Ryan Smothers for your hours of formatting, technical assistance, cover design, wise suggestions and faithfulness to the project. Without your diligent work this book would not exist.

- Karen Steinmann and Ken Smothers for your editing and proofreading skills.

- Beth Smothers for all your hours of technical formatting and final polishing on this book. You were beyond instrumental in getting this project over the finish line!

- Joel Lowry for investing hours in our discussions of new covenant theology and disciple-making. Your input has helped shape much of the material in this book. Chapter 14, "Purity in Christ" is taken from a sermon Joel preached in the Fall of 2019.

- Dustin West and Justin Johnson for field testing this material with college students and co-workers. Your practical suggestions have been indispensable.

I am grateful for the many authors and communicators who have shaped my life and understanding of discipleship. These are just a few of the people who have inspired many of the ideas in this book:

- Wayne Jacobsen (*In Season; He Loves Me*)

- Neil Cole (*Organic Church*; *Church 3.0*)

- Henry Blackaby (*Experiencing God*)

- Bill Vanderbush (*Reckless Grace*)

- Jonathan Welton (*New Covenant Revolution*)

- Stan Newton (*Glorious Covenant*)

- Harold Eberle (*Father-Son Theology*)

- Jack Taylor (*Cosmic Initiative*)

- John Wimber (Various teachings on the Kingdom of God)

- Myles Munroe (*Rediscovering the Kingdom*)

- Bill Johnson (*When Heaven Invades Earth; God is Good*)

- Malcolm Smith (Various teachings on the Covenants)

- Dudley Hall (Teachings on Grace and the New Covenant)

- C. Baxter Kruger (Teaching on Trinitarian theology)

- Brian Zahnd (*Sinners in the Hands of a Loving God*)

- N.T. Wright (New Testament theology)

- Dallas Willard (*The Divine Conspiracy*)

Finally, I am grateful to those who have impacted my life through the years by living the life of a disciple in such a way that it caused me to embrace the call to make disciples of all nations:

- Ray English for consistently investing in my life since we met each other in high school (over 40 years ago). You are a faithful friend.

- Sam Douglass for believing in me as a young youth pastor and inspiring me to be a disciple-maker.

- My *Experiencing God* group— Bernie, Lester, Ken, James, Don—for showing me what authentic Kingdom discipleship looks like.

- Dan Davis for igniting a passion for unity in Christ among fellow pastors in a city and region.

- Robert Mearns for sticking with me through thick and thin and modeling what a Celtic Kingdom lifestyle looks like.

- Lonny Poe for being a trusted friend and fellow pilgrim on the journey of learning to live loved.

- Papa Jack and Frieda Taylor for intersecting Lesa and me at a critical time in our lives and displaying to us what authentic spiritual parenting looks like.

- Tim and Diana Timmons for pioneering the way. Your message of "Jesus plus nothing" has been a game changer.

- Tom Cavazos for demonstrating what it looks like to *live loved.* Your faithful serving models what it looks like to advance the Kingdom both at home and abroad.

- My Sozo Church family for endeavoring to live out better covenant discipleship as a family on mission.

NOTES

CHAPTER 1

1. Henry Blackaby and Claude King, *Experiencing God: Knowing and Doing the Will of God,* (Nashville, TN: LifeWay Press, 1993).

CHAPTER 2

2. For an in-depth treatment of each of these six lenses see Steve K. Smothers' *Seeing Through a Better Lens,* 2019.

3. Brian Zahnd, *Sinners in the Hands of a Loving God,* (Colorado Springs, CO: WaterBrook, 2017), 63, 50.

4. Ibid., 15.

5. Jonathon Welton, *New Covenant Revolution,* (Welton Academy, 2016), 2.

CHAPTER 3

6. Jonathan Welton, *Normal Christianity,* (Shippensburg, PA: Destiny Image, 2011), 16.

7. If you'd like to listen to the "Normal" series by Steve Smothers and Joel Lowry, download them at sozosmtx.com.

8. Mike Breen and Steve Cockram, *Building a Discipling Culture,* (Mike Breen, Second Edition, 2011), 18.

9. Mike Swider with Rusty Lindsey (WTSN), "Discussion on Retirement, Legacy and What's Next," December 18, 2019.

10. Larry Kreider, *Authentic Spiritual Mentoring* (Ventura, CA: Regal, 2008), 46-57.

CHAPTER 4

11. Trey Kent and Kie Bowman, *City of Prayer* (Terre Haute, IN: Prayer Shop Publishing, 2019), back cover.

12. Steve K. Smothers, *Seeing Through a Better Lens* (Steve K. Smothers, 2019) 138-142.

LIVING LOVED Part II

13. Wayne Jacobsen, "What do I do to Live Loved?" (Transitions, part 11, Recorded in Tulsa, 2009). Jacobsen was the first person I ever heard use the phrase "Live Loved, Live Free, Live Full." I'm grateful for his wisdom and insight.

14. Ted Dekker with Bill Vanderbush, *The Forgotten Way Study Guide,* (Pittsburg, PA: Outlaw Studios, 2015), 5.

CHAPTER 5

15. See Appendix B for a fuller explanation of why I chose to use *The Passion Translation*.

CHAPTER 8

16. Brian Zahnd, *Sinners in the Hands of a Loving God,* (Colorado Springs, CO: WaterBrook, 2017), 101.

HALFTIME

17. I'm forever grateful to Robert Mearns, my Celtic friend, for investing in my life.

LIVING FREE Part III

18. Graham Cooke, Foreword in Jonathan Welton's *Eyes of Honor* (Shippensburg, PA: Destiny Image, 2012), 15-16.

CHAPTER 11

19. John Mark Comer, *The Ruthless Elimination of Hurry*, (Colorado Springs, CO: WaterBrook, 2019), 66.

CHAPTER 12

20. Alan Hirsch and Tim Catchim, *The Permanent Revolution,* (Hoboken, NJ: Jossey-Bass, 2012), 39-42.

CHAPTER 13

21. Jonathan Welton, *Eyes of Honor* (Shippensburg, PA: Destiny Image Publishers, Inc., 2012), 44-45.

CHAPTER 14

22. Quote by Joel Lowry in his November 24, 2019, message at Sozo Church, San Marcos. Most of the ideas on purity in this chapter are taken from Joel's excellent message *The Way of Love.* It can be downloaded at sozosmtx.com.